PASSIVE INCOME IDEAS 2020:

How to Make Money Step-By-Step from Zero to $1,000,000 and Achieve Financial Freedom

Dylan Webb

Table of Contents

INTRODUCTION

Living on an annuity ... having a passive income... passive Income... lying on a beautiful beach with a cold cocktail in your hand and doing nothing even while you sleep ... that's what comes to your mind, right?

Nothing wrong with that, but you must understand immediately that living on an annuity thanks to passive Income, being free financially, means "only" that you can afford not to be always productive and no longer have to depend on professional Income.

It means having total control over your finances and time, but it does not mean exactly doing anything from morning tonight.

It means doing what you want when you want, having a lot of free time ... but it doesn't mean doing anything anymore.

Personally, it is for these last reasons that I began to explore the economic and financial world many years ago when I learned that the key to living on an annuity resided in the concept of passive Income.

Then it took me seven years of great effort and many failed attempts to learn how the "system" worked, then to master it until I had full control over it.

That full control that allowed me to change my financial destiny definitively...

Passive Income may not be a definitive status because it may limit some passive income opportunities in time. Therefore you need to be aware that it may be necessary to update your passive income sources even when specific results have been achieved.

Those who think they can continuously stay with their backs in the sun from morning to evening just because it generates passive Income can safely stop reading ... because they are delusional or because someone has told them that it is so!

Therefore, it is clear that we are talking about a happy problem!

So, let's start talking about making more money without working than how much you can make by using.

Passive Income: What it is and why you must have it.

Like many other people, initially, I thought of passive Income exclusively as something that, once activated, would work and self-regenerate without my intervention.

I found this idea heady.

The idea of traveling around the world and beaching myself on many beautiful islands while money did everything by itself was what attracted me most ... too bad that all this, precisely in these terms, is not so easily achievable.

I want to be clear, you can certainly live on passive Income and live very well ... but this requires work, "maintenance," and, at times, the need to regenerate or recreate sources of Income that could run out.

Of course, much better than working in a factory or being enslaved in an office for little money... but you have to know this is not everything, and it is not always a perpetual automatism.

The critical point of passive Income is that it allows you first to free up your time from work and dedicate it to doing things that are more profitable despite being less demanding.

Is it clear?

Most people who have freed themselves financially and live on Income thanks to their passive Income do not spend all day on a Ferrari in Montecarlo or on a beach in Polynesia (these are the visions generated to fool stupid people...). Still, they spend time making their passive income sources work and studying new opportunities or taking care of their passions and hobbies.

Therefore, remember that the beauty of living on Income through passive Income consists of freeing your time from work and dedicating it to more interesting or much more profitable things.

Suppose you have the ambition and courage to think about getting out of the work income scheme creating Passive Income. In that case, you have to know that when you succeed, when you can live on Income, you will live a great life, mainly because you will be able to do only what you love or are passionate about.

When passive Income supports your living standards, you will also want to do something with a higher and nobler meaning and purpose. You will see that it is so...

Writing books, traveling, learning, creating startups, spending more time with your children, doing good works for those who need it, helping others to do what you do, you will find your highest purpose ...

Of course, you could also spend more time making more money, but this will become an option, a choice, and no longer necessary.

Is this fantastic, isn't it?

To get to this, believe me, it takes commitment, learning, dedication, and you need to gain the right experiences, even making mistakes.

The Law of Passive Income

There are many possibilities to access passive Income, and I don't think someone can innovate something in this sense; likewise, there is no hidden secret. Who says the opposite ... only tells lies!

I want you to understand how profitable business is generated, how the economy and mainly finance works.

Let's start with the basics of establishing some general rules about living on Income and Passive Income.

Money is generated where a real value is created.

Value constitutes an advantage/benefit/result for people willing to pay to obtain or use it.

This approach looks very simple, doesn't it?

It is, but most people don't seem to understand this whole passage.

Whenever someone receives money, it means that Value has been created and decided to buy it. Therefore, the first thing you need to focus on is the creation of Value.

Even an employee creates value by moving goods in a warehouse, registering purchase orders, or doing calculations for payrolls. Then, the employer buys from him those services that are valuable to him.

The employee is paid according to a simple formula: Income = Time x Value.

Time, however, is a limited resource (6-12 hours). For this reason, everyone tries, knowingly or not, to focus on the second variable, the value.

How?

Yet, in the end, even if you reach the maximum earning potential for your Value, Time will always be the limit.

Time will always limit your Income because it is not expandable, and you cannot create it as you can for Value.

So, what can you do?

First of all, you have to understand this: the value consumed only once or rarely is never high enough.

You are precious. Your time, your job, your knowledge, your experience, everything has value. Your employer or your customers (if you are a professional or an entrepreneur), pay to get it.

If you are an employee, your value is always equivalent to the same Income...

In reality, even if you are a surgeon, a lawyer, an artist, an engineer, or even a baker, the value you create is often consumed only from time to time and quite rarely. You can only sell one loaf of bread at a time to the same customer. You can only sell one open-heart surgery to one patient. You can only follow one divorce for one client...

Is it clear?

So, you have to understand that one of the critical principles of passive Income is to break this relation to create a value that many people can use simultaneously. I can repeatedly sell that.

People create value, but it is not necessarily those people who sell it or provide it.

A human being always creates value. However, who says that it must be that human being to provide that value?

Some human beings, undoubtedly capable, have created value by creating Google, but it is certainly not them who provide it. They are not the ones directly providing you with the results of a search or a map.

Your landlord worked to buy the apartment you live in and also to find you as a tenant. Now that you have chosen his value, however, he has to do nothing but receive monthly compensation for the amount you have selected without providing another apartment.

Again... if you create something for which you can ask for a "monthly fee," you will have generated value only once so that you can continue to receive a passive income automatically.

You start to understand, don't you?

Passive Income is not free money.

Therefore, you can define passive Income as those income-generating activities that are not dependent (or are marginally dependent) on your commitment in terms of time.

This is very nice, but ... to create such a value, it takes effort and time!

Therefore, we can speak of living on Income and real passive Income only if we have separated (or at least significantly reduced) the proportional relation between the time spent and the money earned. In other words, the gain must be very high, not necessarily in an absolute sense, but compared to the time spent.

Now I think you have correctly understood the concept, haven't you?

The three types of Value to consider when living on an annuity

Selling Value

The term "sale" probably does not need many explanations and is associated with situations where the value is transferred only once (or very rarely) in exchange for money. Any professional activity, for example, is a way to sell value.

This is not optimal in terms of passive Income because once you sell a service to a client, you cannot immediately resell the same benefit. After all, it will take time to do it, and, in some cases, it may no longer be possible.

However, suppose you use the same skill/experience to sell a service to make, for example, a book or a digital product (e-book, video course...), then, perhaps with a marginal cost. In that case, you could sell more and more times your value without having to do it directly.

Renting Value

By renting something, you can generally avoid the degradation of its value or reduce it and obtain a passive income. You have to be aware that, if you rent an apartment, the amount you are offering is not the home in itself but the refuge, the comfort, the security...

The more value you give to these items, the more money you can get from that property.

Earn with an Indirect Value

The indirect value is similar, as a modality, to the sale or rental value but differs in some substantial respects.

To cut it short, let's give an example here too...

Imagine creating a successful blog in which the value is made up of the information it contains. Readers pay nothing to get this information, but with this blog, you have created a powerful form of indirect value: the attention and the favor of your readers.

Therefore, you could rent this value to advertisers, who regularly pay to be visible to your readers.

Is it clear?

Now that you know how to create value, you must look at each of them' cost/benefit ratio to select how to make your value. You must create or purchase resources that offer Value "automatically."

In other words, if you want to build a plan to get to live on Income, you have to consider what you can create or acquire to have a value that can be quickly and repeatedly "transferred" to others with as little work and time as possible.

This is the meaning of the term "passive": obtaining Income by doing as little as possible, the bare minimum.

As we have already said, there are many ways to do it, but all of them fall into the three categories mentioned before.

So, let's go into a bit more detail ... would you like to?

Digital products, software, info products, photos/videos/music tracks...

This scope includes many elements, from electronic books to images and online training courses. Therefore, it is a matter of creating a digital product that has value.

Why digital?

Of course, if you create handmade sweaters, you do something very nice, but you can't merely duplicate and sell them. Also, you have to pack and ship them. Nothing is wrong, but this means there is a relationship between work and Income. We have already seen why, compared to living on Income, this is not ideal.

Digital goods, on the other hand, are infinitely and simply duplicable, and you can design systems (or use online platforms) to provide everything automatically.

Much better like this, don't you think?

Finally, when it comes down to software, today, it is very often an App. You do not need to be a software developer, but you need to contact someone who can create the App, make the necessary updates, and intervene in case of problems.

Blog, YouTube channel, informative material...

I deliberately separated this aspect from the first point because I am referring to indirect value creation here.

Alternatively, if you create a more niche but highly thematic/specialistic/specialized blog, you can operate on affiliations. It is about offering links to websites and getting paid when people buy them through these links.

You have to consider that this is passive Income only when the time you spend writing the contents is minimal compared to the earnings or when others report the contents for you, but you enjoy the benefits.

For example, some have involved the writer in their projects, so they only have to spend their time on SEO (positioning on search engines) by detecting the keywords to have the right topics to deal with. Others do precisely the opposite. Still, others do neither the one nor the other because they have automated everything.

Does it mean you can automate all this? Yes, all this is now almost entirely automated.

Sale of real products

As we said earlier, there is nothing passive in this unless you can create a fully automated business, customer service, and shipping included. If you want to examine this in-depth, get informed, for example, about dropshipping activities.

These are just some of the ways to achieve passive Income.

As mentioned at the beginning, even if you free yourself financially, it is not sure that you can completely stop operating because some passive income opportunities are unfortunately limited in time.

Furthermore, more than half of what people try to do does not produce results. In this sense and concerning living on an annuity, diversification is your best ally.

Having multiple sources of passive Income, in addition to a professional income (at least in the initial phase and possibly linked to something you love to do), you will have your correct strategy to cover any risk.

CHAPTER ONE

What Is Passive Income?

Passive Income has become famous for many people who are tired of working 9 to 5 shifts. Different sources have defined the term differently. Besides, it leads to confusion about what this form of Income is.

Some people confuse passive Income for Income with no effort. Although this may be true in later stages, it does not apply in the earlier step. This is why. Here is why.

The passive Income might be achieved when you generate Income without engaging directly in hard work.

That means that even if you don't work eight hours on your venture, revenue is still generated for you.

This does not assume, however, that you can bring in revenue without doing anything. During the earlier stage, you have to do the real job yourself.

So, you might ask, what is Passive Income?

Here's the stuff you ought to know.

The money you earn without spending much time is what you call passive Income. For some, it is an investment; for others, it is royalty.

That means that you first invest time and money in a company.

If you are working and going, your Income will be created even when you don't spend too much time. In other words, create a system, let it work for you, produce profits from the process, and find the way to freedom.

That's how you let money work for you rather than cash.

What is passive revenue? It's the money you earn if you work hard right now and make it later.

One of the most popular ways to do that is to build a company, enforce the process, pay people to run the company, and sustain revenue.

Although some individuals acquire business from the beginning, others begin to grow smaller and later with higher incomes. When the company expands, you let the money work for you even as you sleep.

After defining what passive Income is, it is also important to note what it IS NOT. For a more unobstructed view, here are some examples.

Sidelines producing side income are not equivalent to Passive Income. Let's claim that you keep a blog site and earn it. You cannot gain passive revenue without promoting any ads on the website through affiliate marketing.

On the other hand, wage increases are also not regarded as Passive Income. Although additional profits are produced at the same time, you still must operate for a particular duration. An uptick is just an increase in an employee's Income. Consequently, passive Income is not equal.

Since having established what may be passive Income and what's not, you have a clearer picture of the path to financial independence. And may it assist you, like many others, along this highway.

There are two main income categories: active and passive

Passive Income

Passive Income from businesses, leases, dividends, or other undertakings in which an individual is not actively engaged. He used to write the book once. His publisher will print his book, and the bookstores will then market his book. He does not have to be involved in selling his book, but he still earns a regular income.

Active Income

percent Total profits in return for a person's services. It includes wages, tips, fees, and earnings from companies and jobs in which he/she is involved.

The money works for you because of passive Income, rather than fighting for your money. A minority of people are surviving on passive Income, and almost no one is affluent.

Many people live on Passive Pay. They are expected to trade for money in their time. Most people work from eight to five. And many others have odd work to earn a fixed income. Most active income earners hardly have enough money to retire and have to work their whole lives. We are constrained and robbed of time by their work. We have no financial freedom and no freedom of time.

Their profit ends if they stop working.

Will you earn an active or a passive income?

Unless you want to be rich, you understand you still must gain a passive income.

Personal finance gurus are always speaking about how you must have enough passive Income to outweigh your expenses to become financially free. That's good, but what's passive Income, and how are you getting it?

Their purest form can categorize profits into four categories: Income gained, investment income, Passive Income, and Leveraged Income.

- As you probably figured, earned an income is money that needs you to pay. Money is made from your time and energy. Many people earn their living as an employee.
- Asset income is interest, capital gains, and dividends resulting from the holding of inventories, mutual funds, and bonds.
- Leveraged Income was created by earning more money with bigger audiences. For example, a speaker in a conference can do as much to organize and give 20 people a speech as 1,000 people but can receive much more money from the larger group.
- Passive Income needs an initial investment and continues to pay for it while the necessary participation dissipates. The first created a cash machine, which often brings money, even if the turnout is minimal.
- You could tell from above, earned Income pays you only what you put in. In other words, it takes your time and your time. You can receive bonuses and promotions, but the sales are limited because only one of you is there.

On the other hand, with passive Income, you can create multiple income streams, which will continue to generate money long after you have worked, when you continue to add more and more money sources, the passive income and asset flow increase.

The Truth About Passive Income

If you're searching the Internet for "passive income," you may find one or two examples, but most of them are websites that attempt to sell you on the day-of-day Passive Income. We agree it's frustrating. We don't know about you, but we research before I leap in any chance or take a trip. There are plenty of excellent opportunities. But let us talk about what passive Income is and, most importantly, what it is not until you start to spend money.

Webster describes passive Income as "from, linked to, and in which the shareholder does not have immediate control over profits." Don't think the whole story tells that. The passive Income is cash you regularly earn without much effort (not to mention that we didn't say "any job"). It's different from Income earned because you don't get money for your time (like a job). But you can also have immediate control of your profits depending on the passive income source you choose. But later I'm going to get to that.

Why would you like to earn passive Income? Okay, this is the significant disparity between the wealthy and middle classes, as Robert Kiyosaki describes in his book Rich Dad Poor Dad. The wealthy invest their money in different streams of Passive Income. If your passive Income exceeds your expenses, you are financially free. "Financially secure" means you don't have to work a day to pay your bills. And then you are "free" to do anything you want!

What Passive Income Isn't

What passive income does not mean until we ask you what passive Income is, first? Let me remind you that it is not? Low Income is not the same as "residual income." Residual Income is cash that you regularly receive once you've finished your job. TV sitcoms are the best example. Some actors are getting "residuals." The actors are paid to shoot the show. Many performers are then paid every time the series repeats. Salespersons that sell services, products, and recycled items (such as insurance) will sell the product and earn a fee from each sale by offering consumer renewals. Book and music publishing royalties are also available.

Some claim that multilevel marketing and network sales generate passive Income for you. Guess what? Guess what? This is also residual.

If you have a small business, this is NOT a passive income, even if you make a lot of money. If you get a paycheck from your job, the money is earned. Nonetheless, there is a way to make this passive income-so stay tuned.

You know, we must claim that it can not be passive Income to start your platform. Whether you sell a product (such as an eBook, a seminar, or other information) or a service, your website will continue to be promoted. You must do this irrespective of whether you offer your goods or can sell other products. Marketing your website is easy. It's not a job, though. And once the marketing efforts begin to go off, you can make a lot of money with little extra effort. But this is residual, not active, in my novel.

What Passive Income IS

What Passive Revenue IS Massive Revenue is a lot? The first thing that comes to mind, and we agree that the most famous example is immobilization. If your investment property has a positive cash flow from a home, business property, or apartment, that is passive Income. Passive Income is also when you rent rooms in your home. You must set it up once, and then the

Income comes every month. Savings accounts, Bonds, and financial-market funds interest income is passive- the bank pays for keeping your money in those accounts. If you have a website that features banner ads and Google AdSense ads, it can also be considered passive.

When you invest in but do not run a company, your profits are called passive Income, precisely what Webster meant when he wrote the concept.

What about the company? Okay, it depends on how you configure it. Rich people build companies and develop a system that the company follows. So, if the owner goes on vacation in Fiji for a month, the workers obey the plan, and the owner still gets the Income. Of course, every business would start with a lot of work, but if you take the time to set up a company to generate reproducible results (just like a franchise), these profits will be passive. And any salary you receive from your business is considered "earned," but profit is considered "passive," according to the IRS. It is essential to work with an accountant and a lawyer to set up your business to help you most financially.

What else would the passive Income be termed? How about self-storage, parking garages, and dry cleaners! They all need some time to start, but once set up, you get money back and forth.

Residual vs. Passive Income

Rest and Passive Income Active and passive Income are like relatives. Both are very similar, and most people regard them as synonyms. Nonetheless, what does it matter? Both are great ways of getting cash into your hands month by month without selling your time or independence. How could it get better?

Reality Check

Be wary of anyone who claims that passive Income does NOT require work. Passive earnings mean no jobs! When you invest in a corporation, a stock, or an immovable property, you will have to do your research (called "due diligence"). The study is work! Work is work! You will also have to control your savings, track their progress, and adjust when necessary. This is work too! This is work again!

The real kicker is that research and administration is only a part-time effort. And this work can be done most of the time from almost anywhere, including on a beach in Fiji.

Don't forget about the FUN factor. I'm sure some of you read this still enjoy their job (if you still have one). Some of you have a company of your own-and I congratulate you! But most of us work simply because we must feed our families and pay the bills. Looking at passive revenue streams and spending your time and money will produce many, many revenues. FUN is to look for and execute your passive income plans to fulfill your dreams. It's FUN every month, week, or even every day to get money. And checking and handling your money-if you have something to handle-is FUN.

Passive Income is income, whether you work, sleep, or play. Passive Income The American Internal Revenue Service, determines profits from "trade or business activities in which you are not interested." Examples include:

- Rental Income from real estate
- Profits from companies that do not require direct involvement or participation from the operator
- Royalties from book publishing or selling intellectual property
- Profits from internet advertising
- An insurance agent, for example, may gain a residual income when its customers renew insurance policies.
- However, Income goes away if the insurance agent leaves the company.

When you invest in a networking or multilevel marketing company in which you must continue to earn an income, that is not a passive income either. If you want and still earn income, you can stop working together, which is passive Income.

The big myth about passive Income is that you're finished when you buy or build an asset for you. You may feel that you don't have to spend or manage more time on it.

The reality is that there are different degrees of "passive" employment, for example, but the property may be too time-consuming. Usually, when you buy a property, there is an initial stabilization process, ranging from making repairs to locating and testing new tenants. Once the property is secured, you can sit and get rental checks for a while, but the occupant either leaves or the water heater fails, or a tree falls on your house, and you must spend time on the property once more.

This is not the same as a deposit certificate at the bank where you receive it, and that is it. For example, when you know what you're doing, the rental property's actual profits are much higher than the deposit certificate's potential revenue.

Know how passive and residual Income are unique and how exactly "passive" an asset is. Why is passive income essential?

Imagine if you had no job, wife, family, state, or anyone else to rely on for money. This form of Income can provide you with.

Across various traditional financial planning models, you are encouraged to find out how much cash you need to withdraw. You spend that money on retirement. This strategy has some serious shortcomings. What if you live longer than you expected and save your cash first? Secondly, what if you would like to leave it after putting so much energy into saving that money rather than spending it?

PI > E If your Passive Income (PI) is more significant than your expenditures (E), you are entirely free to choose how to use your time because your resources continue to pay for your lifestyle, whether you are working or not.

The reality is you don't need to be free of debt to be financially independent, pay off your home, make a ton of money, or become a millionaire. You need more revenue than expenditure.

It's that easy.

You may choose to stay out of joy and freedom instead of obligation or debt. Passive Income allows you to have more choices.

What if something awful happened and you couldn't work anymore, on a more serious note? How are you going to pay your bills? You also have more peace of mind when you have enough passive income.

This equation has two components. You can increase your passive Income to become financially independent quicker, and you can also explore how to reduce your expenses.

So how are you getting more passive revenue?

Two main types of passive Income exist. Passive investment income is the first type. You need funds to invest in these income instruments to earn passive investment profits. If you have funds to invest, you need to rely on analysis and due diligence to decide which of the passive tools best suit your situation and perception of risk.

The second type comes from creating a small or no money own income vehicle. For example, you may be opening a website that produces ad revenue or joining a network marketing agency that allows you to continue receiving Income when you are no longer active. Or you may start your own business or become an affiliate of another corporation.

If you already have money to invest, you can probably generate profits faster than anyone who doesn't. If you don't have any money to invest, you should give time, energy, expertise, capital, imagination, or all.

Sources of Passive Income

It is difficult to find income sources today. There is a widening gap between rich and poor. Others claim you always have the Income to survive when you work hard. But what are you going to do if it's challenging to find a job? Even the rich find it difficult to keep their Income. Nonetheless, for those who know where to find sources of passive Income, this is less concerned.

Let us, then, first describe passive Income. What are passive income sources? Income sources have various forms. Some familiar causes include earned interests, dividends, sales, land, equipment, cash, and rent.

Dividend

The dividend is received from a company's Net Income. It is a way of sharing Income and is more prevalent in the stock market. If more than one person owns a company, the payment is divided according to each shareholder's assets. This owner is called a shareholder, and a dividend is referred to as a profit. Money or stock can be the dividend. It is a cash bonus when bank checks pay the gain in cash. And it is a portfolio dividend if allocated as stocks or bonds. The tip is also an attractive source of passive Income, especially during the growing period. Not all firms are paying stable dividends. It is important to remember that the selection of stocks determines your future revenue. If the chosen business has shown higher dividends, it will be highly likely to continue. Income stocks are named some firms that consistently make higher dividends. Revenue stocks may not be large corporations. Nevertheless, even some large companies fail to make regular dividends because of their high operating costs. Not all stores are, therefore, sure that they are one of the sources of passive revenue.

The "capital inventory," which relies on a pleasant industry environment, is one of the many income sources on the stock market. For example, any IT company can be a candidate as a passive income source if the IT sector is beautiful. This suggests that choosing such businesses is safer than selecting a large company facing economic turmoil in the market. Therefore, a vital sector business is a good source of passive Income in the stock market.

Interest Earned

The interest earned is also popular as a source of passive Income. Our money collects an interest rate if we deposit our money in a bank. What is the quality of interest? The interest rate is the amount paid when we borrow money, and when we borrow, it is received. While we're not a creditor, we can make it because the money we deposited in the bank adds to the lender's amount loaned to the lenders. Before we see our deposits as sources of Income, there is a requirement.

We may consider our investments as a source of passive Income. It occurs only after the market rate is high, and our investment is considerable. Time deposits and bank bonds are examples of liabilities. A savings account can also be one. Banks vary in interest rates from each other. To obtain attractive Income from the banks, we should choose the right bank and deposit when the interest rate is high.

Rent and Lease

Lease and Rent Passive income sources are multiple and dynamic. However, lease and rent were the simplest. Without a doubt, everybody knows that our Income is proven to give us a stable income source by making our property leased or rented. If you have a new house and a lot of an apartment unit, you only need someone to take place. Your sources of passive Income here are not your land but a stable tenant who can reliably pay the rent and stay longer. The only factor here is your tenant's profile. If the property is a commercial estate, you may have to rent a bar, a gas station, or a warehouse to those businessmen. Your tenant's profile here is more reliable than the household. Commercial lot tenants are certainly going to stay longer. This can be your company because this kind of investment is not liquid. It is an investment in the long term. Nevertheless, many of us will consider this as one of the most reliable sources of Income.

Nonetheless, investment in transport services is hardly regarded as one of the potential sources. The threat here is high. But if you are just an average person who owns one or two units of a taxi, lease them out if you are spending a little on your car's depreciation.

Sales

Sales Business Buy-and-sell may be sources of revenue depending on the services or goods you sold. That your company, the more passive your Income is. It's an advertising and a good source of adequate Income when we exchange smaller things. But if cars, houses and lots, stocks and bonds are what they buy and sell, they are significant sources of passive revenue.

Land

The land is the most significant source of revenue. It doesn't need to be rented out. It has been the most secure source of Income since time immemorial. In the past, fertile soil can grow without human intervention crops, trees, plants, and grains. Also, livestock and poultry were fertile land commodities. All these items that land can generate are passive income sources. Until now, but with little interference, these conditions are still valid.

Equipment
An owner of a rice mill will get a certain amount per bag. After the harvest season, the rice mill owners ' cash flow is much healthier than farmers '. Rice mills are hardly needed in the post-harvest season. Some other crops and grains are, however, required by other equipment. Shelling devices and graders are at the front for peanuts. Dryers, farm tractors, and grinders are different forms of machinery on the farm.

Equipment is one of the best sources of passive Income, even in the region. Can lease heavy construction equipment to contractors and builders. If you are an average person, you can buy a dealer. A dealer is being leased. You are gaining from your sold products. It's a passive income, though, because it's your computer that works for you. The printing press is the most common and most heavily rented equipment in the region. This is a company and an investment at the same time.

Now we see that there are a lot of income sources. It's wise to invest it in something that gives us Income to spend, rather than spending so much money on consumption. We should save our active Income, and our passive Income is the one we can invest in. Our wise choices are, therefore, also sources of Passive Income.

Passive Income Opportunity in Stock Trading

Many people will agree that the best opportunity they can have is an income opportunity. That's why everyone searches for it. Yet, it could hardly be noticed by some. It does not necessarily involve much effort to get the chance. The lion is a good analogy. Following ten tries, lions get their prey. They will have used all their food by the time they kill their prey. Your diet is just enough to replace your lost energy, and that energy is just enough to take another day off. On the other side, crocodiles float on the water, wait for their prey, and never let it go. They'll be full and not hungry for a long time after their meal before finding another live victim. The latter is the best example of how to get a shot. And this example is like a passive income incentive in terms of income opportunities.

A careful examination of the economic situation impacting the danger-reward ratio of a specific investment method can be used to consider passive income opportunities. When you invest in the stock market, the right option is if the price of a business you are willing to purchase is at its lowest level. In this case, it is cheap, and the stock valuation value is high. This is another forum for passive Income. In the stock market, we benefit from a company's dividends and, at the same time, from its appraisal. Taking use of price fluctuations provides some incentives for passive Income. Ideally, they buy shares at low prices and sell them at low prices. This also applies to nearly all trading instruments. When a clear and robust pattern emerges, a passive income potential becomes apparent. To make the correct entry, we should understand why these changes occur to monitor the market's course. One instrument's price action is essential to know to determine the capacity and limit of a passive income opportunity. This is determined by the changing market conditions guided by numerous different factors, from which we also have to learn profoundly.

Traders use two methods for assessing a passive income asset, which is known as essential and technical analysis. Fundamental analysis is a tool for analyzing current economic factors affecting consumer behavior. When the financial situation is excellent, it promises positive investment growth. Traders are, therefore, ready to buy attractive devices. And by doing this, they force the other market players to raise their prices. But if the economic situation is worse, concerns are triggered, known as an aversion to risk. The latter is referred to as risk appetite.

We can calculate economic strength and weakness using periodic economic indicators. GDP is one of the most famous symbols of the economy. When the GDP number is higher than expected, the economy is stable and investment-friendly. The unemployment rate is another important indicator. Consumers are reluctant to spend when the unemployment rate is higher. Industries are struggling. And so, it's a lousy investment moment. This is just one example of the importance of each information for traders to make a sound decision. Good economic indicators also provide investors and traders with a passive income incentive.

This economic news can affect the feelings of the consumer. Nonetheless, rumors often make traders respond more than the information. Most traders, therefore, buy stories and sell the news. This is also another area for passive Income. How does it work? How does it work? For example, if a company were to launch a highly competitive product, investors would purchase the business a lot earlier. The value of the company would, therefore, also be lower. And if the news isn't real, early purchasers will sell and benefit. Knowledge thus provides us with a passive income incentive.

The use of technical analysis is another approach that traders use to define a passive revenue opportunity. Technical analysis provides traders with historical graph data. The graph may display trends that allow traders to follow the market trend. It also signals that a trading instrument's value exceeds a certain point where a reversal happens. A passive income potential starts when the graph shows a clear trend right after a setback. Experts in this field have various instruments for disclosing a passive income chance. Price is shifting within a trading range here. If the array is disrupted, however, it means a significantly stronger pattern. This is considered a "break-out." A breakthrough event is an excellent opportunity for passive Income. The purchasing of an explosion has proven lucrative.

Regardless of whether fundamental or technological approaches are employed, there is always a passive income chance.

There are still other ways of finding passive Income, such as new trading instruments. These include the IPO, public bond sales, and any new investment instrument issue. In summary, because it is a new problem, the price is lowest, and there is no way to go up.

The initial public offer (IPO) is a new share problem for the growth of a business. Companies need not borrow money from banks to expand their operations. Instead, they would search for investors to collect their funds to finance the expansion process. The new problem has still not been sold on the stock market. When a company executes the IPO, investment banks buy the new stock issue. Afterward, investment banks will pay for the company. Then will sell the current item purchased by the investment bank on the stock exchange trading floor. This form of sale in the store is known as an IPO. Why many investors want to purchase an IPO is that most of the businesses that issue an IPO are expanding. When it develops, a company grows, and potential growth is active in the near term. The IPO of a growing company is also sold at the lowest price. The market path is therefore set to a bullish pattern. Will trade that shares after the initial public offering. Such dividends will become secondary stocks if they are passed from one investor to another. IPO is an excellent example of passive Income. Rumors about an IPO increase risk appetite on the stock market. During the economic slowdown, IPO is hardly seen except for the sector to which it belongs. A passive income opportunity begins when the economy is continuously growing, especially if the company that issues the IPO is the primary beneficiary.

Fusion and acquisition also create a passive income incentive because investing in the giant is always enticing.

We saw many possibilities for seeking passive Income. If you are still not determined to try one on your own, people who specialize in trading these instruments also have a passive income opportunity. You can ask fund managers for advice. Many high-net-worth people invest in these traders ' proven talents. You can study the way they do about passive income opportunities if you choose to do so. It is also wise to invest in people who already benefit from Passive Income.

CHAPTER TWO

Ideas for Passive Income

Most of us know that every amount we receive is revenue. We work to make money, and the more we live, the more money we get. But if we also make money because of our Income, we might feel it's a corporation. This is a much more general concept. If we become more precise, this form of revenue should be called passive Income.

The most desirable Income that everyone wants to enjoy is passive Income. It's because we earn less with less effort. As a human being, our energy is minimal. We depend on payment based on the energy equivalent that we use. In school, we learned that everyone ought to have ideas about any job to gain. Later on in our lives, we understand that passive income ideas are essential ideas that we should have.

Those people who are not happy with their current Income must look for some ideas. We can try a lot of income ideas. Small companies can provide us with profits. The challenges we still face are the challenge in determining what to spend, when, and how to do it. We should also invest in innovations, in other words. It can be expensive to know more. Nevertheless, the outcome of our ideas can create significantly.

Small businesses, such as a start-up restaurant, are one of the most popular passive income ideas. You can first handle it yourself to set it up and to make sure it works well. You can also gain experience. You don't have to cook or serve customers, however. You may hire someone to run the process. The secret to a significant income is investing in people. The integrity of the people you can recruit is all you have to remember. Trusted people in your business will guarantee your profits. But, if your restaurant is too small, you must get on with it. In this situation, the company is still in the first phase of income generation. If your restaurant attracts more clients, you can invest in more employees. It is better to invest in individuals than to waste additional time. If your restaurant income covers overheads, it is unfair to spend your time and resources

Retail companies like a convenience store or a pharmacy are nearly identical to a restaurant. These are also some of the most common passive income ideas. It takes time and energy at the start-up stage. You continue to be as safe as it develops. You will measure your monthly stock sales. Today, because most retailers use POS technology, it is not that hard to do so. This lets you track the takeoff of your products every day and the cash flow. The bills and the stocks available are not to be counted manually. You must also make a physical inventory annually. But it's infrequent. In the meantime, if your retail business is successful, you need to start up because it is risky to depend on just one unit. If your company's location becomes a weaker environment for your business, you can also close your retail outlet. However, the risk is divided and reduced if you have several branches. Every branch of your store is a single portfolio. Therefore, expanding the portfolio is one of the most influential passive income ideas.

If your business is a restaurant or a retail company, you can still draw more Income from the same client. "Franchising" is one of the proposals of passive sales in retail companies. If your restaurants or retail stores prosper and become famous, other entrepreneurs will own or be part of the same company. This can be done by franchising. Individuals who have no business experience can purchase a franchise. What you should do is give them the help they want.

How is franchising functioning? You will earn Income with less interference if you are an ordinary shareholder. Invest the necessary capital for a specific time, including the franchise fee, and allow the business to run with the leading company's assistance. It is only the continuation of their activities from the perspective of the critical company owners. Other investments accomplish the growth of their market. They can receive a franchise fee because the name of their businesses works for them. A franchise lasts between two and five years. If you want to set up a restaurant, you can compete and join the franchising's big chains.

Even if your company has grown so much, there are still more passive income ideas for your business. You can also earn Income from pure revenue from shop sales to franchising by listing your growing company on the stock market. You can make passive Income by valuing stocks. It is the name of your business that is marketed in franchising. It is the company's investments in the stock market. Both are beneficial since they mean expansion. In other words, the selling of assets is the franchising or stock exchange listing. Passive income concepts don't have to come from various types. You could have different income ideas in the same sector.

Nonetheless, you can still explore various other income ideas, such as real estate investments and online companies. What you need in real estate is enough money. You can earn revenue by renting your property.

More ideas on passive Income, like web hosting, e-commerce, and affiliate marketing, are available on the Internet. Affiliate marketing is currently the most popular phenomenon. Ideally, to start an online company, you don't need big money. Sometimes no amount of capital is required because some processes are available. Blogs are examples. You can create a blog free of charge but can use it for your online strategy. The submission of articles is also open. We spend most of the time creating a website for money. There are now some cheaper or even free sites. The price is only covered by using other technology to boost the plan. Some people use some computer robots or other plug-ins to automate their companies. It will be cheaper to publish your book online if you want to. What you must invest in online business is your time to create everything and your creativity to develop new strategies. Continuous training is also a help.

Retrospectively, we don't have a new retail market. But if we continue to innovate, we can create a new idea. Online companies are always impossible. You will develop a new environment, a new business, a new type of life, and some new ideas for passive Income using existing ideas.

Online Passive Income

In the past, it was beyond everyone's imagination to make money without resources or effort. We assume that luck lies on our side. So, if we learn that we can now win online money, we can hesitate to believe. Several people recently tried to verify it out. Not long ago, online foreign trade was one of the most popular trends for earning some money on the Internet. Some worked, and I was apprehensive because they needed to learn about some fake brokers' activities. But we could find more reputable websites where we could trade and make money if we searched the Internet carefully. There are, therefore, many people who have even started to invest in a small amount of money. Some beginners may have suffered some catastrophic losses. Some may have invested more equity and began to make others money. Anyone who has pursued this cash-making method is undoubtedly fascinated with passive digital revenues.

Amazingly, you can make money on the Internet. There are several ways to generate passive Income online. The most popular trend is now the promotion of affiliates. I heard these words; the first thought is, if not a fraud, that this is only another online selling arrangement. We should spend our time, money, and resources in such an online business's start-up process. And usually, we've got to do several things. Anyone who can promote or sell the site owners ' goods will also wait for anybody who can do so. But it's different from trading on the field. The promotion of partners does not pressure anyone to work outside their house. Although you need to create a website or blog, enter the most forums, and market posts, it is not permanent because your websites do the rest, when everything is set, as the robot serves his master.

Digital passive Income is created when a digital service is purchased. But keep in mind that you should only upload an original piece for once because any submission to another website of a version of the same item is called spam. You may write a similar spun paper. We can insert some links in our post, which can guide visitors to your blog. Your articles ' contents will not have to appear as a sales text. It should be helpful so that it can draw more tourists. The contents of the reports could even determine the traffic. Visitors who may type similar words in your materials will see your items in the search results using successful keywords for optimizing search engines. The purpose of the product marketing should be to transport traffic through your articles to your page. The more tourists you bring to your places, the more likely it is that some of them can buy the advertised items. You will earn a fee for each purchase they make.

Another approach to creating passive online revenue for affiliate marketing is to enter those forums. You must discover and stay on your niche so that you build your reputation to gain your visitors ' trust whenever you talk. Yahoo response is a good step in driving traffic to your page. All you need to do if you enter their forum is to answer the questions and to show the guests that you are an expert. For starters, your niche is about cooking, and you promote and sell some e-books. You need to search for and answer questions about areas of interest. If you suddenly get more interested in visitors who asked questions, they might check your profile. Will show your connection to them openly. Don't put a link in any of your responses. If you respond more, you can somehow add a link. But it's essential to provide the visitors with your response and the answers they need.

The Twitter post is another way of driving the flow of travelers. Search for and follow more blogs of renowned personalities in their niche. Don't forget it doesn't matter to the post. Readers should respect you in your field of expertise. When you build your reputation, you and your reference can be followed by readers. Blogging can also help you get the search engine performance score.

Usually, the search engine results can not include a blog post or an article you make. Some keywords you contain for optimizing the search engine in your posts, it doesn't seem to work for you. It is, therefore, best to access several forums on several high-ranking websites. You must apply any reports to them if necessary.

There are different ways to break up a passive online income. You can only start earning if you have some traffic on your website. It takes time and energy to make it happen. In the first step, you are just beginning to build a profile that can draw visitors to learn more about you and your products. Therefore, creating a passive digital income is not an easy task because it often takes a long time. Here are some useful tips:

1) Don't count on just one post. Submit your papers to all the folders of things you know whenever possible. Consider all your things almost the same, but not the same, to maximize the search engine.
2) Choose a brand not released on the market yet. Popular products will always be subject to fierce competition. The best outcome, therefore, does not always have to be popular.

3) Build your website or blog. You are going to drive the traffic here. If your site has a platform for users, you can use it through email marketing.
4) Be a participant of specific popular sites. Whether or not a website provides a forum depends on your quest. Nonetheless, some places do.
5) Look to your target. Look for your market segment. Think of anything relevant to your field of expertise. This is where you should base your selection of products. Look for some interesting topics you can always relate to before determining which brand you wish to promote and sell.
6) To discover more pages, keep searching. There is something to offer on every website.

The above tips are just a reminder. When you continue to seek ways to make passive digital Income, you may discover various things that may benefit your online business. Social media marketing and network marketing are some other ways that can support you in your online business.

Passive online Income can also be passive or active. It is not easy to look for anything that could give us less effort in terms of revenue. We may define passive Income in terms of time and effort versatility. Usually, we cannot note that passive digital Income we know is associated with online work. As many people believe, the Internet's payment is because your Income is earned without leaving our house. There's nothing wrong with spending so much time online. In most instances, you must pay a long time in front of the computer screen.

Nevertheless, we can still consider such Income a passive digital income. It's not how long you should do things that determine the essence of passive online revenue. Alternatively, it's mobility. Until you're stuck in a job, you could produce a passive digital profit. The only form of internet income that is not considered inactive is a wage for online jobs.

Both people will look for a passive digital income eventually. There will undoubtedly be too much traffic on most websites at that time. Now is the best time to start your business online and one day make Passive Income online. Work today. Work today. Gain one day. Gain.

Make Passive Income Online

Everybody wants to be rich. But not many know that perhaps their definition of "rich" is a little bit out. One must have "passive income" to become rich.

What is passive revenue?

Passive Income is Income you get even if you don't work. You can still earn passive Income in addition to your employment, or you can stop working and live off the passive Income you earn. For example

a) After the initial research process, Blue Chips will make dividends from their investments without much effort or effort when you invest in Blue Chips.
b) You open any franchise stall like McDonald's and can run your McDonalds franchise system without running.
c) You have some legal MLM in place (not even illegal ones), and you either must try to persuade enough people to convince other people or buy your products or services. (You don't see your franchise owner in a cashier or to serve you your Big Breakfast, do you do?
d) You are an insurance agent, and your customers annually renew their policy.
e) You have properties and lease them out every month to receive payment.

The list goes on, but right now, you get a sharp picture.

So, you know, yeah, what the passive Income is, what's the hell?

I know of some of us (including me) dislike maps but can not clarify the value of passive Income any easier. The general idea is to earn what is known as "active employment" when you come from the quadrant's left side (if you are an employer or self-employed). In other words, you swap MONEY TIME. You may have a career with a high income, but you need to exchange your other interests with time and discount.

On the other hand, you earn EVEN on the quadrant's right side if you don't work. The most comfortable check for those who are confused between a business owner's difference of self is to ask themselves if you transact time with money? You are self-employed if you own your food stall selling burgers. You belong to the Right of the Quadrant if you own a franchise with a proven system (like McDonald's, you will remember that they train all their workers with "Welcome to McDonald's, have you here or take away?").

To show how highly valued passive Income is, people, buy only passive Income for residential properties! Don't underestimate passive Income, even if the value isn't as high with active effort as you can get.

What Make Online Passive Income?

And yeah, passive Income still matters. But why the Internet? Why the Internet? Even the examples above can provide me with passive Income.

The answer is not hard: if you want a "vehicle" to gain passive Income, you want the most value, and the Internet has:

1. Unlike property investment or Blue Chips, you don't need significant capital.

2. You may remain anonymous. You don't have to make cold calls or threaten friends and family for legitimate multilevel advertising, which often makes relationships more challenging.

3. You can operate wherever and whenever you have a computer/laptop (or even a high-end telephone) and Internet access.

4. Your target audience is the world of the Web, and even if you are an introvert, you can project your business idea to the world.

5. You can always check the search engine, blogs, comments, and posts to see if your actions are a scam or not. If there are reports or no news about the system you are considering, it is probably a scam. You can't shut the thoughts of the entire internet world. There is thus less risk of being scammed on the Internet, as opposed to popular belief if you know how to do your investigation compared to the world outside, where you have limited ways of doing your research. (If somebody asks you and tells you about a legitimate multilevel

marketing system, there is little research information on it. Just because somebody you're asking doesn't mean that it is a scam; it just means that they don't understand it. In comparison, if the whole world of the Web is quiet about the online program that you will participate in, it's awful, and it isn't.

6. Many online companies let you cash out whenever you want without limitations, i.e., you cannot sell your blue chips whenever you like without considering the economic rates.

Top 5 Passive Income Ideas on The Internet

A vision shared by millions of people allows passive internet profits. The idea of building a website, offering an item, service, or information, and then sitting in and watching the cash flow is undoubtedly attractive.

However, creating a passive income is another matter because it takes work, perseverance, and determination to make it work. For everybody who sits back and watches cash flow, hundreds of others are also struggling to make their websites successful.

But, when they start with the best passive income ideas, everyone can create a consistent flow of benefit. Building on good, tested arguments for passive Income can help you build wealth on the Web in the long term.

The fundamental principle behind creating a passive income is to find or to create a product or service that can be purchased many times over several years. This implies that the product or service must be attractive during this time.

The best ideas for creating a passive income follow. The word "passive" is perhaps a little misleading because all profitable websites now and then need a little research. Nonetheless, when you try to construct your passive Income, it is easy to follow one or more of these concepts.

1. Blogging

Blogging By default, blogging should not be considered "passive," as new content needs to be posted frequently. But once you create your audience, it becomes relatively easy to manage your website. All you need to do is keep a schedule of new content frequently and respond to commentators. Most popular blogs only take one or two hours each day, but they could collect tens of thousands of dollars during that time.

The trick is to select the right niche or themes that are broad enough to bring many people together but are narrow enough to make your blog an authority over the topic. When you find the right subject between those extremes, you will have a reliable website for passive Income.

2. Affiliate Marketing

This is perhaps the most popular method of passive internet income.

The great news about affiliate marketing is it doesn't always take up any cash. All you need to do is register on one of the many thousands of websites selling your products or services. You get a fee for each sale that is usually a small percentage. More and more sales you make, of course, the larger the benefit.

You need to pick items that best fit the subject of your post, posts, or another type of website. The goal is to build enough customer traffic when you start to make purchases from your associated goods and earn a lot of month after month.

3. Apps

Apps are a multi-billion-dollar investment known to anyone using a smartphone. It is now simpler than ever to develop an app, although the complicated will have a design team. If you can come up with and create some fantastic app concepts, you can earn significant Income daily.

The main thing is the idea. It must be patient, easy to use, and addictive. Games are the most common types of applications, but they are also the most expensive. Nonetheless, if your concept is sound, a single excellent app idea, you will earn big money year after year.

4. Article Writing

Many websites allow you to publish articles on virtually any subject. For example, Squidoo and Hub pages need no money or set up other than fill in a registration form. Besides, you can subscribe to business partners from outlets like Amazon. The more people you read your posts, the more money you can receive from your selling affiliate goods.

You will nevertheless have to write several helpful, interesting articles to draw the attention you need. Many of the most successful writers who use those websites receive a few hundred to a few thousand dollars a month.

It means that at least over 100 articles and possibly many more must be published to achieve these goals. But it is possible and does not cost your cash, which makes it almost no-brainer to write for these pages. Like other passive income ideas, the subject you choose is broad enough to touch a large enough audience but limited enough to be considered an authority.

5. Photography of the stock

Do you like to take photos? If so, you can generate Income by uploading your pictures to one of the numerous stock websites for photography. They are shown on these web sites, where you receive a small payment on each approved photograph if they are deemed good enough.

This approach can take a little time and may not be chosen for many of your pictures. But every month, you get a decent profit after you have created enough stock images. If photography is your passion, it can work well for you because it does not need any capital and can be built over time.

Those are only some of the best passive income ideas that you can use over the years to produce a healthy income. Remember that the essence of passive Income is creating a design that attracts and sells enough people again and again.

CHAPTER THREE

Generate Passive Income - It Starts with the Right Mindset

Most people are asking me about passive sales. But why all the interest in this subject right now? Now people look for passive income chances; either they have lost their homes or are looking for more income sources, maybe their company has slowed down, so people are looking for new ways to generate Income.

Very often, the same people who seek passive Income are the same people who seek debt relief. Sadly, though, the two definitions don't fit together so well. Therefore... The goal is to get out of the debt (payment of the mortgage, amount of your car loan, etc.) by whatever means is available. When you concentrate on debt collection, you don't focus on making more money! Here the two concepts collide. Making lots of money is the critical principle of passive Income, whether by generating additional revenue, for instance, or starting a business. If you want to create a passive income, don't focus on debt relief... That's going to take care of itself!

You want these things included in your credit report, as this helps to improve your score (I suggest keeping your credit card debt below 30 percent). If applying for loans or credit lines, people will look for these forms of account.

It's all about getting into the right way of thinking. People are stuck in what I like to call a consumer's mentality and a wealthy thought. Wealth creators aim to produce passive Income. Consumer thinking is about 9-5 jobs, security, debt relief... All the things you feel, but disguised as protection, not real freedom, offer you financial freedom. This will hopefully give you some clarification about which side you want to move on.

Being out of debt won't help you get more money because nothing can get more money or expand your company.

You must also look at the value of cash on time. Pay your home will not help you create passive Income. You may have seen some of the mortgage acceleration products on the market that pledge you to pay off your mortgage for 30 years in seven years. First, the number of people who do this is less than 0.01%! One explanation for this low rate is that you must pay more every month from your wallet to get your mortgage delivered within seven years. You use clever calculations to make it look like you don't, but you pay more every month. Even with less interest, you must charge, and you have to have extra money.

You give up the money you have available immediately, but remember, that's the wrong way of thinking! You can put this money into passive Income, into your business, or increasing your passion. Focusing on debt release holds you bad longer!

So you have a fixed mortgage period for 30 years. You do two things when you pay it off with one of the 7-year acceleration schemes (and note that less than 0.01 percent of the people who purchase these accelerator schemes do so and get their mortgage repayments in 7 years!!!), you screw your credit up. You need at least one mortgage in your report to be able to leverage recognition properly!

You lose the value of time for cash.

You save 5 percent a year now. But the critical thing to keep in mind is that you give up extra Income to pay off this loan faster. Instead of saving 5 percent, you can make 20 percent, 30%, 40%, or even 100+%. When you look at passive Income, you also have to worry about one, which would yield less than 10 percent! For Instance, if you want to begin a network marketing agency, start with real estate, etc... That stuff gains more than 10 million Total! There are resources there that increase much more-you will learn how and where to find them!

So, you lose money! So, you lose money!

Let's see an example... You take a $100,000, 30 years fixed mortgage on 1 August 2009. Payments of interest shall be $536.82 a month. Pay that amount, and 30 years later, you have paid off your loan after you have charged around $93,000 in interest over the period.

You will have to increase the monthly payments to $1,400 to pay off within seven years. This reduces the total interest you paid in the term to just under $19,000.

How many people can afford MORE THAN DOUBLE their mortgage payment? The response is less than 0,01% based on statistics of the people who choose this7-year accelerator choice!

Even though you could... Better ways to use this money are available... Yeah, you know it: OPPORTUNITIES PASSIVE!

For example, even with an average 20 percent return on investment-and trust me, 20 percent in the world of passive incomes is MUST conservative! -let's say in the case above that you can afford $1,400 a month.

Your mortgage payments are set at $536.82 a month. Would then invest the surplus fee of $863.18 in a passive income vehicle at a 20 percent return.

Investing a minimum of $10,358.16 ($863.18/month) annually over 30 years, to a return of 20%... Your investment is only worth 9 million dollars* after the same span of 30 years!

If the estimate is only applied for seven years... Your $863.18 monthly investment is now estimated at $173,750 in seven years. This far exceeds the $74,000 that you would have saved if you had embraced the brand spirit.

As you can see in this case, you lose money to provide this additional security. (* includes 3.1 percent inflation, 15 percent tax rate). If you want to create extra cash, it is NOT the way to pay off debt! You must focus on my two core principles: mastering the ability to access capital, Investing that money wisely. The best place to invest your money is to invest in yourself. Invest it in your relationship!

Building Passive Income as an Established Marketer

As a proven marketing manager, you are likely to have the stuff to get more passive cash overtime automatically. It's only a matter of putting together the pieces of the puzzle in an effective way.

The first step is to store what you have. What items have you? Can websites or domain names be open to you? What are your skills, and what kind of experience in internet marketing have you developed? We are sometimes so satisfied with what we have that we ignore our potential. I did it a lot.

Occasionally. Look through the brand list and say, "oh! I've just marketed that once or twice, and it's perfect." I'll then find ways to give old products a new life. . can put it on the own domain, create affiliate interest, recycle content in a new place, etc. It was a Jimmy D. Brown mentor who taught us to get everything you can from what you read to use it to make the most of it.

I want you to do that as a first step. Talk about how you can turn it into a passive income stream— or to ramp up what you're receiving passively right now.

One mistake that. See, most internet advertisers is that they only put their products on sale at the Warrior Forum. That's just taking you so far. Users won't see the brand after some time (unless it's the key term in the search engines that works). Bring it on your territory. Give it a new life, a new promotion, and a unique opportunity to earn your money passively.

In some instances, the items you have produced may be taken and used as list builders. This is something. Intend to do right now. In return for people's email addresses, the older (still valuable) items are a freebie. This becomes a passive income earner, where it hadn't been before.

Review the sales letters you have also run. Are they just as good as they could be? Sometimes it can have drastic benefits to spruce up your sales letter (contact us if you need spruce-up, have low updated notes, and generally help conversions).

Remember where the goods are for sale. You miss out if it's just a regular PayPal button. Most products will do far better with the support of their affiliates. Using JVZoo or such a payment gateway, you will have a much better chance for members to sign up to promote your product.

Networking is, of course, a big part of the game. When people know you and your work's quality, it is much easier to get affiliates out there. If you don't get enough leaders, it's time to work on your strategy. . have excellent partners, but. Could use many more for good passive income. This is undoubtedly something. Must do.

In addition to the sale of more items, a broader inventory is drawn up. If you don't create a list while selling products, you are incomplete. If. Think about how long it took us to link the two. It makes us grumble. . have heard of big promotions for people as Warrior Products of the Day, but they didn't build a database with it–thousands of opt-ins are gone!

Blogging for Passive Income

Do what. Said above-use old products as freebies to get more people to subscribe to your list. All work together to help you raise more money.

Most advertisers have a home page, so you ought to. People are reluctant to build a blog because they think it is so crowded. But it doesn't matter at all to me. Nobody else has the same experience and the unique insight to share. Believe it's good to have a blog on a similar topic, no matter how many others do. If nothing else, it works as a kind of therapy to get your thoughts and feelings out of marketing.

It can help you sell your products, build your list, build confidence in you as a person, etc. You don't have to spend a ton of time doing it - think about it.

Active List Building

In addition to seeing some of the passive income sources die. I also profoundly regret not being more active in the listed building. Active List building

It is so rewarding to sell to and build a relationship with those on your list. You can gain a high passive income when you set up an autopay series that operates hands-off when people register for your list. Many members of the own list came from sales of the products and forums, but. Could have done much more over the years. Be vigilant with the advice and make a list building a passive income goal.

Membership Sites

Membership platforms are another perfect passive income beneficiary-depending on how you perceive it. Despite those marketers who try to sell you as passive and straightforward, they are not always. They are very gentle and patient to proceed.

They're great because you don't always have to go to find new customers. The customers are there when subscribing. We will be satisfied if you provide interest.

Consider putting some of your previous products on a membership page. Think about a topic that people will want to hear about every month. The new affiliate page is Writing That Rocks –I offer two monthly issues on writing issues. It's not something I've encouraged much beyond the own list, but it's an excellent little people who love membership, but it's transformed into passive income (if you don't take time to write the new questions!). In this situation,' tolerant' means that. Don't often find new customers for new products-autopilot membership renews. For most membership pages, this is valid. It's not a passive, hands-off earner.

Upsells

Upsells. Talked a lot about stuff that. Wish. One of those things is that. I did not use upsells for too long. If. had them, just felt like I'd annoy people. Okay, some may be angry, but. Think many more are thankful-at least as. Do. . Tend to offer upselling that is very useful and topical. They're not too expensive, and they're not just about getting the money of people-they're about to be beneficial.

When someone buys the product these days, it usually goes upselling. This is not something consumers are forced to do, and it generates additional profits, hands-offs.

If at this stage you did not add upsells or set up a real sales funnel, seek. You may be shocked by the increase in your salary.

Cross Promotion

Cross Promotion By the same token. I was often timid about the promotion of the material... Wasn't meant to be! It's no shame to let people know of the other very precious products and services. Yes, people always thank us because they let us know what additional items are available

Look at what you sell–do you sell it to customers as a one-off, or do you allow them to learn you sell something else they might like? You can even see this among famous Amazon writers–the intelligent ones let people know they have other books for sale. This can boost your passive income significantly.

Passive Income as an Affiliate

You can even build a portal to keep your items up to date.

You are an experienced marketer, so you probably have gone into affiliate marketing at this stage. If you're like me, you're disappointed with updates from Google and anything, and you may have let things fade a little. Get back into the game! Get back into the game! If you do things in the right way (as Google always liked), it's still possible. Are now revamping all passive partner sales after. I have scraped many of the frustrations.

Some things have always succeeded and. I Always feel they will. The first is high-quality material. Google wants to serve the content that its searchers want to see precisely. And you must give them that.

Another thing that has always served is keeping up with trends-including, including the famous "release jacket." It is easy to start a mid-mega affiliate and make sales through your blog or other web sites. Give it a passive income attempt.

How Can an Average Person Generate Passive Income?

An average person can, in many ways, produce passive income. Within his experience, even without trying to start high, getting some extra income is possible.

The salaries are essential to us. But apart from our wages, we can make a decent sum out of what little money we have. What we do first thing we need to do is save money. Saving money calls for discipline. There is a lot around us that pushes us to buy what is beyond our immediate need. We should accept that we need enough resources to produce passive income.

We're all puzzled about how much is enough. As we increase our profits, we always spend more. This is the greatest challenge in producing passive income.

We don't automatically save our hard-earned money to raise the requisite investment capital. What we need is to quantify and evaluate the costs of our day-to-day needs. We decide what we should focus on often. Many have forgotten the first thing to produce passive income. Whenever we get our salaries a little, the money will become significant over time. It's easier to say than to do. But that's not a difficult thing to do. The generation of passive income should be our priority.

Typically, we assume that passive income can only be produced by significant capital beyond our limits. Maybe it's real. If we continue to believe so, it is accurate. Everything is possible these days. Long ago, we had to budget large amounts of funds because the minimum capital required was also high for virtually every investment type. The internet now provides numerous options to produce passive revenue.

We will begin trading on the stock market if we have at least $2,000 or less. When you decide to invest a little in the stock market, the dividend won't be lucrative, regardless of how good the business is. Nevertheless, by buying and selling stocks, you can produce passive income. Trading stocks involve a threat. But if you are aware of the fundamental tools for managing risk, the stock market is fascinating and optimistic.

If you are cautious and willing to wait long, investors with little capital can choose a managed portfolio such as the mutual fund. You can put your money in a mutual fund and pull it out whenever you like. Nor is the minimum capital significant. Your savings are paired with the money invested by many individual investors. This capital is used to invest in different investment funds. You can produce passive income by stock valuation and stock dividends in the portfolios of the fund. When the fund grows, you will also have cash.

Today, if you are a greedy person who wants to benefit from a volatile market's potential profit, you can also exchange currencies for as little as 500 dollars or even less. You must be a carrier kind of shareholder who bet on a long-term trend in bulls and receive a currency rollover while enjoying your value or floating gain to generate passive revenue. But this is only valid in an excellent condition on the market. It doesn't mean you can't earn here. Yes, the most profitable ability for financial trading is the maximum leverage. What helps this sector is a deep understanding of why a currency moves in a single direction. In other words, it requires skills. This is the easiest way to generate passive income, on the other hand. It is also the liquid market in which you can invest.

Nonetheless, this is the least active of all kinds of passive income. Investment here is neither market based nor currency. Everything depends on you and what kind of merchant you are. To generate passive income here, you should first try a demo account before investing in a live performance to test your trading strategy.

Nevertheless, many of us still use the conventional way of generating passive income. You can set up a food cart company or buy a car for a taxi. If you already have a small apartment space, you can lease it. You can purchase some inexpensive sports equipment or set up a fitness center in your neighborhood. Business is by far the most common revenue source. The problem is that most people are trying the same thing. Competition thus becomes much more stringent.

A food cart company can be a very profitable way of generating passive income. A lot of food carts line up inside the malls. You may feel that such a business is not permanent. Surprisingly, the number of these small carts has increased. It's not difficult to operate such a company. As it is small, it is simple to work, and costs are lower. It's selling like hot chocolate, though.

It's as easy to operate a taxicab as ABC. The perfect scenario is when you own the taxi system, 100%. This alternative income source is suitable for those with at least one fuel-efficient car already.

An average person who has owned a small house and lot or an apartment can lease it for passive income. The proceeds from the lease can be used to pay another housing loan. This is a long-term investment program. We can make a sensible decision to use our assets to produce passive income for more continued investment. Using them to earn a living can be short term, as our property loses overtime. While land value is valued, structural maintenance is expensive. Otherwise, tenants may come and go. You also need to be more innovative in using your things.

It can also transform your land into a fitness center. Sports equipment gradually depreciates. Many people are insane about health and fitness nowadays. There is a substantial market for this, and it has been continually growing. When our world is more stressful, people are increasingly anxious to cope with stress. Such a growing demand is a good chance of producing passive income. When your clients pay for the resources they buy, the less they spend is paid for.

There is a wide range of online companies from which you can select. Your imagination is what online business needs. Everyone here does all to bring people to their pages, pushing us to think of better strategies. Although competition is intense, there is ample space for development. The important thing is that you can continue with less capital and less risk at any time.

Therefore, choices are always open for an average person looking for an opportunity to produce passive income. Let's not overlook which first we must study what we will do before we start. Everything is possible everywhere and every time for everyone.

The mindset of The Passive Income Earner

Many people are still outdated and conventional in their thinking when it comes to jobs. As many have learned, a well-paid career means either spending extra time in the office or stressing your stiff work muscles. Most of us have this common notion of gaining more, and we must always sweat out our asses.

In this age known as the knowledge generation, people slowly awaken to the vast potential of more gratifying efforts. There are more business opportunities than before; both the small and large businesses draw more and more entrepreneurs. Homemakers who were once confined inside their homes can now think of virtually every possible scam and scheme for gaining money—

from advertisements about cooking them and knitting them on the Internet to write and publish novels and books. This looks like many ways to help people earn more while working less than doing more to make more. The World Wide Web serves as an oyster shell that offers the increasing numbers of passive income earners of our age a thriving market.

But what does passive income mean? What are the examples of services and activities that can provide us with these revenues? How can we get passive income?

Passive income is income that does not need your direct participation. Leasing, profits on artistic work or invention, and internet advertising are typical examples of passive income. If you want to earn more but work less, you should start creating income courses in which you do not engage directly. If you want a company of your own, think of a business model that generates more passive income. Therefore, personal and financial independence as soon as you have expected. Passive income is the best way to add to your current job and finance.

TWO Stealth Forms Earnings AND A 3rd Variant Form

Over time, residual income results from work performed either on a one or with minimal maintenance.

There are many ways in which a broad range of organizations can produce residual income. It may be annual revenue from loyal customers or purchases from new buyers. You may not be interested, such as an online book sold on your website, or have some personal interactions, such as an insurance company informing consumers of renewal fees. The job required for this form of passive income is typically something that can assign a subordinate. The residual income is not entirely like recurring revenue in the sense that it can still require your participation, such as a monthly fee coach or therapist, or the benefit that a caterer receives by delivering food to a local institution. Although recurrent incomes of an active kind provide stability, your earning potential still depends on your capacity for personal growth.

Leveraged capital, on the other hand, uses others ' jobs to generate income for you. You make money out of other people's labor instead of your own in this form of passive income. Leveraged income can or may not always be residual income, but in turn, you build a powerful template to raise your revenue to higher levels further.

The third type of combination is a switch in the second type and is called actively leveraged profits. Although not passive theoretically, this form of income is crucial to earn more and work less. This needs your direct participation, but you will make more money if you have more people involved.

Events such as symposia or conferences, individual classes or seminars, musical recitals and concerts, and events and other parties are among the most famous examples.

Although you are a direct participant (as a facilitator or sponsor), your income is much higher than a paid natural hourly rate. To explain this more clearly, fill a room with a thousand people paying sixty dollars each, and all operating expenses are covered, and the return is still good at the end.

*** What is your current attitude?

Okay, step one is not to think about leaving your daily job immediately because it takes a few jobs before you can work off your passive income and leave9-to-5. Work to slowly grow one or more of these passive income generating companies, which will allow you to escape from the rat race and live a life of which you have only dreamed.

Consider your opportunities and choose from the many ways in which can produce passive income. How could you make money out of other people's work? Can you conceive of a product that is not only purchased over and over by people but also sold by others?

The days are gone when you must work harder to earn money. It is already a past time when labor and profit are the two sides of the money equation. For passive income, even when you sleep, you can make much higher earnings.

CHAPTER FOUR

Learn Passive Income Secrets That Can Change Your Future

Ask hundreds of people if they would like to increase their wealth, and all 100 of them will say yes. But ask them if they're "grave," about half's going to shrug. Heck, many people's health and even their resources are not "serious," but they're those truly dedicated to change, making a real difference in their lives. The big gap between the poor and the rich is that the rich act (as they dedicate themselves to their richness), whereas poor people are more likely to think about improvement but never take the necessary steps.

If you're serious about improving assets, you're going to want to read this chapter because it's the beginning-where it's going to be all serious.

Yeah, yeah, you're committed. You must be since you still read. All right, let's get to the meat of the problem.

Many have heard of 'passive income,' but few have understood what this means. Passive income is described as income for which you don't need to work. In other words, if you're with your family on a sunny beach, you can still earn money. The secret to producing constant and increasing wealth is to operate on passive income rather than working income.

For example, if you are a doctor, attorney, employee, or astronaut, you don't make any money until you stop working. Your salary at work is gone. You may have a lot of money, but you will make no more if you put on your working clothes, get into a car, and go to work. The wealthy tend to concentrate instead on collecting passive incomes, and their riches expand every day, whether they go to work or to the Riviera to work on their branches. And that's why the rich get more decadent as everybody else gets poorer. And worse. And worse. And worse. And worse.

Fair warning! Fair warning! Don't think it's easy to create passive income-it's not. It takes some work to set up your foundation, it requires planning and commitment to building this foundation, and unless you make a base, there will never be passive income.

Let's think about it another way-this week, you could spend 40 hours working as an office clerk for an insurance company, and in the end, you make $10 or $12 an hour. Yet spend 40 hours working on building your passive income. Each day-even on weekends-you can have that $10 or $12 an hour (or a lot more).

Imagine making $400 in the morning before you get up. Imagine you're getting $50 for dinner. Imagine a week's holidays and coming home to find a $2000 check in the mail. This is passive income. This is passive income.

And how can you do that? Step one is not to stop working your day, for a little work is needed before you can live off your passive income and escape the the9-to-5 era. Passive income creation is a long-term thought, not a short-term, so you must pay your bills. But never forget, the rich are the ones who act. The poor come from work and switch off. The poor come from work.

Immobilien is one of the easiest ways to generate passive income. If, for example, you purchase and rent a beautiful property or commercial building, and your mortgage payment is lower than your rent, you have generated passive income. Of course, the big problem is that most people don't have the vast capital to buy land. Therefore, you may need to -your goals a bit by making smaller quantities of passive income, with far less spending, so that you could work your way later to property investment.

Multi-level Marketing or MLM is a type of passive income for someone who does not have large sums of money to spend. Although people are afraid of MLM schemes, you have to know that their operating methods are not like infomercials before getting into it. You don't just enter an MLM system and start to make hundreds of thousands of dollars immediately. If you know somebody who has made it big at any time in the MLM market, they would probably sell in long, strict hours. This is a significant drawback as most people don't like to buy. The easiest way to generate passive revenue is to find a real company that does not need sales.

Nonetheless, successful companies produce consistent and significant passive revenue without selling hassles without the hundreds of thousands of dollars necessary to go into the ground floor. If you want to make passive income for yourself and your family, starting small and building a strong base, then take the next step and see the following6-minute video. Multi-level Marketing or MLM is a type of passive income for someone who does not have large sums of money to spend. Although people are afraid of MLM schemes, you have to know that their operating methods are not like infomercials before getting into it. You don't just enter an MLM system and start to make hundreds of thousands of dollars immediately. If you know somebody who has made it big at any time in the MLM market, they would probably sell in long, strict hours. This is a significant drawback as most people don't like to buy. The easiest way to generate passive revenue is to find a real company that does not need sales.

Nonetheless, successful companies produce consistent and significant passive revenue without selling hassles without the hundreds of thousands of dollars necessary to go into the ground floor. If you want to make passive income for yourself and your family, starting small and building a strong base, then take the next step and see the following6-minute video. Note-take action from the powerful. If you want to increase your money seriously, you do too.

Creating Passive Income

Personal growth is like all else; time and effort are needed. That opportunity can be challenging to come if you work 12 hours a day. We also wanted to take this opportunity to talk to you about what you do and what you could do. You're probably working your ass off to support yourself and your family right now. You and your loved ones can be a big grind to this 8-7 job. Have you ever stopped wondering why you were doing that? We bet that if you force yourself to ask yourself the next question,' what else can we do?' Well, year in and year out, you will continue to do the same job every day, do the same thing hour off, and then start the process again. Or you could follow a different path, and this route generates passive income, perhaps tax strings. It's not as hard to support yourself in doing the things you love.

Let me prove passive income for the first time. Imagine if you're going to have a thread, and the yarn is over a bowl. We can fill the bottle by letting the line go down one drop at a time. It is a prolonged process, but we are indeed progressing on the positive side. Still, what about adding another thread and doing the same thing? Now we have two strings, and we add twice the water we used to be. So we have to add more lines until we have a nice flow to get the bottle full. That's passive revenue and substantial financial opportunities.

Don't get me wrong; we've got to have little working bees out, and we're always going to. There will always be people who follow the same direction as all the others. We're not going to frown and glare at these men because it's the reason we can do what we are doing. They will never walk away, and they will always remain in the path they have been taken. Yet people like you, and we feel otherwise. Some may say that we're lazy, that we disagree. We're just saying we're better than that.

Until you speak directly to friends and family about income strings, most people say it's risky. Hmmm, let me share with you a scenario. You go to your 9-5 job one day to find out that you are smaller. You just missed every revenue source you had that way. Now that you are rational, how logical is that to you? Sounds like a healthy strategy for you. You put all your eggs in a bowl and broke the pot.

Tomorrow, you'll be working for eight hours and take $100 back. The next day, you're going to need to get up and do it all over again to get the same $100 back. How much money are you going to bring back then? You don't do anything on your day off if you are like other men. But what if you do it intelligently? Say you can sit down and create a book for 8 hours and sell it a copy for $10. Your eBook now sells a copy a week. You may think that's not a good investment, but we said it a week. After a year, your work lasts 8 hours and becomes 520 dollars. That's over five times what you did at your 9-5 job. Guess you can market this book for years, and from just 8 hours of work, it might easily translate into thousands of dollars.

I know it's hard to continue; you're working 50 hours a week, after all. Let's have a real holiday and a motivated year. You can spend 8 hours a day creating small projects that can earn you $10 a week, more than likely on your holidays. So, you create seven projects and spend 8 hours a week starting a new income stream or finishing another project for the rest of the year. At the end of the year, with 408 hours of work, you will have made over $16,000, equivalent to $40 an hour. The best part about it is that you make over $16,000 when you take the whole year off next year.

So now you've left when you can see now that you can do it yourself. You can now take time and continue to produce more passive income. It has limitless earnings potential. Sometime later, you can earn your salary and turn it into a cord to handle it more effectively, but then work to make more money again.
This system's security is how much you will do if something went wrong with an income flow? The most out of your profits is 10 percent, but all you must do is replace it. This sounds much better to me than being fired from your job.

Now that we showed you the example, let me tell you all the advantages of passive income and income strings.

1. Invest for a while at the beginning and allow the project to generate revenue alone.
2. You pick the tasks, and you choose the hours and days to do them.
3. Your remaining deferred income operates 24 hours a day, seven days a week.
4. All you must do is build another string if you want to make more money.
5. The sky is the limit to your productivity.
6. Have more time to spend time with your family, friends and take a holiday.
7. It can generate passive earnings that are not dependent on another business or economy.

I know that you think, "Whoa, that sounds great, but we need some examples of this passive income that you talk about." Well, those income are simply anything that can be generated after it is setup. Here's some stuff to think about...

1. Knowledge Products-The Internet makes an eBook perfect for people to create, detailing' how-to' knowledge. How to start an online company, buy a car without being ripped off anything that allows people to make life easier?

2. Building software–If you have the potential to do anything more comfortable, more straightforward, or to teach it, and if you have a good idea for a software product, you can have a gold mine.
A friend of mine created a game that educates children about mathematics. He instead sells that game on CD to parents and schools throughout the world. From his initial investment of time, effort, and money, he makes a nice passive income each month. Bill Gates founded the Microsoft Company, which markets the Windows Operating System as the best example.

3. Provision for ads–if you have a website that attracts thousands of visitors every day from the search engines, you may sell a banner or a banner for each month you receive on your page. It is defined once, and the passive residual income is obtained.

- Newsletters or ezines-offer your ezine advertising space.
- eBooks-offer the book ads. Offer the eBook freely or put affiliate programs in it.
- Google AdSense–Position your website with Google Ads. When someone clicks on the ad, each click has a fee. You can receive a significant

monthly income if you have 100s or 1000s of pages on your web.

4. Build a membership page-you can charge a monthly fee for access to your membership site if you are an expert in your field and can provide information, knowledge, and support. The more you win members, the more money you make. You can also recommend other products and services to your customers, from which you receive a fee, as you are an expert in your field.
Please realize that many things can be done to create more time and money in your life. You only must grow from the average person in your way of thinking. Once you do that, the sky is the frontier.

How To Building a Passive Income?

What is the way passive income is created, and how can we be financially free? The starting point varies depending on an investor's profile and the investment itself. Some wealthy investors start by carefully studying the factors affecting their investments — many start by getting acquainted with everything. Nonetheless, most of us do not even begin with a capital. The less money we have, the longer the passive revenue is built.

The building of passive income should start by saving money for an average person.
When time passes, they may understand that they don't receive passive income, but instead, are the lenders. Credit is especially useful for business

expansion. Nonetheless, very few lenders lend to start-up entrepreneurs.

To save money, should reduce the daily expenditures by identifying things we can do without. Sometimes, because it is necessary, we can't help spending. But again, how important these issues depend on us. We should prioritize and set less critical priorities. For those who take passive income seriously, no plans are collected because their mentality is deep. We feel that saving money is a match against themselves and not a simple transfer of coins from one location to another. When you invest, you lose. If you save, you're going to win.

After saving enough money, you'll think about where to put your money. You'd be looking for somebody to help you answer all your questions. Make sure you don't do all he's going to say. It is easier to do your work. You may have a lot of information bombarded, which can confuse you. Don't forget to be fair and filter it. The safest thing to do is to know the fundamental investment that you can try.

The next step in the process of generating passive income is investment choice. You must call a broker if you choose to invest in the stock market. A broker is a third-party company that helps investors search for sellers once they purchase shares. And it is also the one that allows investors to seek buyers when they sell investors. After a single trade, brokers pay a transaction fee... When invested, the cash will be used when trading starts. Your payment is credited to your trading account for your stock purchased. Occasionally can also buy shares without opening a trading account. You can use your checking account immediately after the transaction to pay for your inventory in this scenario. With the advent of technology, any broker can no longer make business easier. Investors can access live transactions via a trading platform. A trading platform is a technology tool for stock trading, and so on. It acts as a broker, too. A broker's role today is to be a guarantor for your businesses. This means that its name is used on your behalf for trading.

Let us now presume that you have already opened a trading account, and your broker has given all the appropriate trading tools. You can now pick an investment company. The most critical stage in creating passive income is that the future income relies on the chosen business. At this point, intensive research is needed. It is recommended that you read the basics of the company. The data you provide is given on the platform a broker offers.

You will find many good stocks in the stock search. When you create passive incomes, the first thing you need to remember is the business's dividend. An attractive dividend business is also known as an income reserve. The stock of income is considered safe. Nobody can tell you if a company is an income stock or not. Furthermore, if your work focuses on dividends, you will know it alone.

One is called a cash dividend; the other is a cash dividend. Through checks, the cash dividend is conveyed. It is issued directly to shareholders. The stock dividend is indicated in the stock certificate. This is not, however, given explicitly to investors. The full number of shares is added to your portfolio dividend. It doesn't fill your pocket right now. Yet your investment is expanding. Whether a prize is cash or stock is voted for at a shareholders ' meeting. You may also attend a meeting of investors because your shares qualify you to vote on it. You can, therefore, opt for it if you want to earn a cash dividend.

Not every shareholder is the same. Some prefer steady growth in investment. Others want money. If you only choose a cash dividend, you can choose another form of stock that can only give cash regularly. Two types of stores exist secondary stocks and preferred stocks. Precisely the one listed above is a secondary inventory. Preferred stock is unique because it does not require you to vote or participate in an inventory. But it is named because the priority is given to preferred stockholders in the distribution of dividends. Besides, preferred stock gives you income fixed regardless of the performance of the company. It is offered at a fixed percentage of 15% from 10%. It does not necessarily mean that the preferred inventory is better than a secondary list. Besides, the secondary stock dividend, although sometimes considerably smaller, may rely on results much higher.

Bond investment is one of the many choices for starting to build passive income. Investing in stocks could be a good starting point to know more. It's fundamental and the most common. You can try a more advanced one once you gain experience. You can then jump into mutual funds or attempt to trade currencies or even futures.

The easiest way to start building passive income is by saving. If we save money, we can always go to a bank to deposit. But recall, the easier it takes, the less we can get.

Therefore, seek what is known and not what is simple is more comfortable. There is no easy way to achieve success. We must take it all one at a time. Passive income creation is not done overnight. Sometimes we don't know our goals, so we change our plans. But never change the game rules. Some things need to be first, and some things need to be last. So, in truth, it is not necessary to limit your choices. The important thing is to be financially free. How to be free financially is to start generating passive income. Then! Now!

How to Develop a Passive Income Stream?

How can passive incomes be developed? Are you interested in creating a passive income stream to add to your lifestyle? You can receive a lucrative passive income source, a list of seven you can use to raise your profits. These are available to any potential contractor. That income opportunity provides a brief overview, which gives you a better understanding of what works for you. You can use one, two, or more ways to produce these revenues. So, let's continue. Let's start.

1. Blogging

Blogging has invaded the online world, and everybody has the chance to be a writer. You can write a blog on any topic you can think of. Here are some numbers from WordPress.com: ·
77 million WordPress websites in the world;
13.1 billion blog pages;
409 billion monthly readers·
38.7 million new posts every month;
50 million comments monthly.
Give you the chance to launch all your passive income sources from a single center. A blog allows you to brand yourself and develop an online presence; it is your gateway to targeted online traffic for your passive income.

2. Internet publisher

In 2015, business owners and marketing teams invested some $135 billion in developing new digital marketing platforms to promote their brands, products, or services. One media source estimated that the site used 25 percent of the entire advertising market — 73 percent of companies planned to increase their Google AdWords advertising budget.

Similar advertisement channels are: · Google ad terms 73%· Bing ads 55%· screen networks 52%· Facebook 52%· LinkedIn 26%· Twitter 24%-smaller social network 18% You can gain a competitive passive income if you are posted on such sites. You can create a significant passive income flow by targeted viewpoints to click and act on forums, blogs, review websites, landing pages, splash pages, and other online networks. The more traffic you aim for, the higher the potential to better click with your ads. Support you market any product or service that produces passive income. With this form of publicity, you must develop focused publicity skills in the area you try to work.

3. Affiliate marketing

The affiliate marketing industry reported $14.94 billion last year, which indicates that it is a very lucrative source of passive income. Using affiliate networks such as ClickBank, Click Promise, the Commission Joint, or other affiliate marketing outlets, you can receive commissions between 5% and 90% of all purchases from other people. You also can create and sell your services through these networks of partners to produce even more revenue. This directs a highly targeted audience to your affiliate landing or sales pages with which you have registered. And this should always be achieved with your tailored funnel schemes, from landing pages to data collection until you send prospects to the affiliate landing page. Or you can use other digital marketing tools to drive traffic through blogging and social media such as Facebook and Twitter to your affiliate connection.

4. Amazon

These days, Amazon e-books outperform traditional publishers and represent up to 20% of the total internet traffic. You will benefit from this traffic and gain passive income as an Amazon customer. If you have a website or blog that talks about a category or product niche, you could earn from Amazon Associates' fixed advertising rate for products sold in a category. Working with Amazon is a relatively simple process and lets you develop your business through your program.

5. Freelancing

Another way of gaining lucrative revenues online is by offering freelancing services; an estimated 20 to 33 percent of the United States' total workforce is independent workers ' volume. Yet companies plan to increase their reliance on freelancers, and almost 50 percent of freelancers recruited last year alone. And the pay for freelancers is also rising, growing by 37 percent year on year. For freelancers, a wide range of skills and expertise are required. Some of the top skills companies now have are: IT and coding· design and interactive· writing on translation· and the smaller niche markets. Thus, it could be a lucrative passive income source for you if you're interested in free trade.

6. Online content author

The demand for digital authors has risen in the meantime, as the search engine algorithms shift towards more focused and quality original content, making it an extremely lucrative source of digital revenue. The online writer's average hourly salary is about $27 an hour, far higher than the federal minimum wage.

7. Marketing network

Marketing network or MLM is essentially a form of direct sales and is also known as person-to-person marketing. You benefit from network marketing by selling products directly to other customers. You can also gain a passive income stream by establishing your network of independent dealers, otherwise referred to as your "network," to give you the ability to earn residual income from different levels of sales and membership.

Network marketing has grown considerably in the last few years. It has become a source of income for many successful network marketers, with around 150,000 people signing up every day for these networking systems. Worldwide, more than 50 million people have joined network marketing companies with worldwide sales of 90 billion dollars. Many people are now using the Internet, developing their network by creating blogs and landing pages to sign up for recruits and then marketing email information. It can build this into a very lucrative income stream, which may allow you the ability to fund your full lifestyle rather than contributing to a traditional job.

CHAPTER FIVE

Creating Successful Passive Income Streams

Honestly, it's a good time to live. I know it sounds incredibly ambitious in terms of what is happening with the state of global personal finances and economies. But it's a great time to live because you can build effective passive revenue sharing and possibly increase your financial security due to the internet. Yes, even in these difficult times.

What is passive income? What is passive incoming?

Let's first be specific about all passive income sources. A passive revenue stream is a way someone produces income from you or your initial investment with somewhat minimal work. For instance, stock and bond dividends could be an example of passive income. Leasing properties are also considered inactive (although I believe that any leasing property owner would take umbrage in calling their work "minimal"). There are all around us examples of passive income sources. The other day I walked down the street and found a laundry coin run. While the profit margins are probably not astronomical, this laundromat generates income from the initial investment with very little labor.

This kind of cash flow generated by this type of INCOME STREAM

typically benefits you in many ways. Individuals with money-making efforts on their hands do not usually give up their primary source of income as they want the financial security that a 9 to 5 type of employment can provide. The advantage is that they can pay off their debts, save for income, and purchase primary and secondary homes with little financial strain. Why? Why? Because it is pure gravity for this kind of money.

HOW YOU Golden retriever Its Online INCOME STREAMS

There is probably an endless number of ways you can utilize the internet to create various cash flows. Therefore, it is necessary to diversify your sales base so that your revenues do not dry up when the demand is there. A few years ago, I spent millions of dollars trying out different deals or services online. The bottom fell almost overnight from that market because companies realized they were doing a ton of fraudulent activity. This will always be a cautionary account for me, a reason for diversifying your various income paths.

Here are the most popular online revenue-generating methods: Affiliate Marketing-In general,
Affiliate marketing is one of the best ways to make money online. Affiliate marketing is used to create a website to display, advertise, and sell others' products. Whenever a visitor clicks the company from your link, you get a sales commission. The significant part is that the organization does not monitor, sort, distribution, and payment of commissions. Nearly any organization selling a product online has an affiliate network-Amazon, INGDirect, smaller Internet marketers.

Blogging and collecting ad revenue — Years ago, people frequently spoke in the context of their AdSense platform about the "hidden cash machine" from Google. It's simple to set up a website, sign up for AdSense for free, put your AdSense code on your site, and make money every time you click on the ad. It is becoming increasingly difficult to earn money from online advertising as people become blind to all these ads on websites. However, it is not uncommon for some people to pull this income stream a few thousand dollars a month. (But remember, the traffic on their websites and blogs is enormous.) Information Products-You can also make money by creating and selling information products. Data items.

Selling Information Products
Most people spend online money because they want a fast response to an urgent request. This is where you can find incredibly useful eBooks, training videos, and podcasts. Once, third-party companies are working hard to deliver your ad and collect the money on your

behalf. (You owe them a small transaction fee this time.) E-junkie is one such page. The most challenging part of creating this type of passive income stream is to make the actual information product.

Develop a referral service

I am intrigued by how people make money online or offline. Create a transfer service. For those who own it, referral services are a cash cow. This is all 1-800-dentist is. In contrast, referral programs are all systems that hook people up with physicians, lawyers, or counselors. Build a product and promote it in your area. Upon reading this, don't say, "I can't." It's perfect to be alive now—-more than ever—-it's easier to make money online. It's ideal to be alive. Thousands of people are unaware of their ability to generate cash through the internet. I know because I was one of them before.

Proven Methods to Creating Passive Income On The Internet

Please read on if you have no idea what "passive tax" entails. It is money you earn passively, which you only need a little effort to make the profit.

1) Online advertising

Online advertising was the best way to create passive online profits. You only need to promote ads on the ad network via your website or blog. Next, you must apply, and you must meet the ad network requirements before they accept you. Applicants should have a page that has lots of content and can reliably drive traffic. If the ad network approves your application, you will add the ad tags you will send to your site and start earning. You should leave it alone and watch television. And take a walk through the park. The ad tags shown on your website refer to your page or blog's essence so that your followers will benefit as well.

Adsense

Two forms of ad networks exist. One is "CPC," and the other is "CPM" (cost-per-thousand-images). CPC charges are based on the number of visitors who clicked on your advertisements, while CPM depends on a full print or the number of visitors who watched the commercial tags. Here are the lists of ad networks you can try to connect to the most popular ad network: Adsense Google AdSense. Adsense can charge you based on CPC or the number of visitors who clicked on your website. You should, therefore, convince your viewers to click on your advertising to receive them.
As I stated earlier, advertisements contribute to your website's essence to convince the reader to click on advertising. You remember these banners on the side of most websites and blogs, that's what I'm thinking about.

Media.Net

Yahoo! Bing Network Contextual Ads is run by Media. Net and is likely one of the second-largest ad network companies in America. I've used Media.net ads for several months, and AdSense's revenue has been very close. The approval process for candidates is, however, much more complicated than Google.

CPM based ad networks

CPM based ad networks ContextWeb, AdClickMedia, Adbrite, Modify, BuzzLogic, and Casale Media are all CPM-based ad networks. If your web site knows how to control traffic, you can receive similar benefits to the CPC-based system.

Ad Publisher Network

Ad Publisher Network Ad Publisher Network is an organization with a 1-2-3 authorization system. They deliver CPM-based ad tags from CPM ad networks and post them on your website or blog. Compared to the ad networks, 60% of the total revenue and 40% for the advertiser are received. The benefit of using ad publishers is that you can instantly get your ad tags within a single day. NJ Network is the only ad network I care about for now.

2) Affiliate Marketing

This is one of my favorite ways of creating digital passive income after spending almost a decade of earning income from affiliate marketing and other partnering methods.

The concept behind affiliate marketing is easy-you earn money online by advertising another company's products for a fee for every sale you make. In theory, all you have to do is a partner with affiliate programs, get their affiliate links, and promote them everywhere. Affiliate Marketing is an excellent way of generating passive income because you can blog/check the items you endorse once and earn rewards forever if readers use your links to click and buy.

Please remember that to create passive income streams online, and you must be willing to spend your time, money, effort, and commitment at the start. So what do you expect? This is the best time to think about your future and to see the endless opportunities awaiting you. This seven-day free training series I will share with you is the right place to create passive income online through online advertising and affiliate marketing.

Create Passive Income Streams Flowing Straight into Your Bank Account

The creation of passive income streams online is not at first, so' passive.' You will have to put some things into motion before you can "passively" sit back and watch the money roll-up. Yet online, I love to earn a residual, passive income, and you like that.

Passive Employment Benefits, 1. Once the initial work is done, setting up methods for generating income could make the payment very' tolerant.' 2. The freedom to work where and when you want.

3. You can earn a passive income 24 hours a day, including while sleeping or playing with your children.

4. The power to' owe' you a pay increase whenever you want... by creating multiple passive income sources.

5. The ability to create a virtually unlimited profit restricts hard work and creativity.

6. After you get a few streams of revenue, it's easy... long weekends to go on those lovely holiday spots that you've always dreamed of.

7. The ability (I love this) to generously give your choice to charities.

5. You will produce residual income for years... even if you can't work.

A) Affiliate Marketing If you have been online for some time, you know that there is a ton of money to make to sell affiliate goods (other products of peoples.) And why not! You don't have to produce the item or collect the money, don't offer support, or discounts, anything... send hot (ready to purchase) visitors to the sales site.
I'd want to offer products that pay a high commission and incorporate long-term tracking cookies (so that you'll receive payments even if it takes your prospect sweet time to buy.) Affiliate services offering multiple "tiers" fees (those who sign under you are paid for the

sales they make) will spend a long time after the initial purchase (sometimes for years). Think of residual, passive income. Affiliate Marketing If you have been online for some time, you know that there is a ton of money to make to sell affiliate goods (other products of peoples.) And why not! You don't have to produce the item or collect the money, don't offer support, or discounts, anything... send hot (ready to purchase) visitors to the sales site.

I'd want to offer products that pay a high commission and incorporate long-term tracking cookies (so that you'll receive payments even if it takes your prospect sweet time to buy.) Affiliate services offering multiple "tiers" fees (those who sign under you are paid for the sales they make) will spend a long time after the initial purchase (sometimes for years). Think of residual, passive income.

b) E-books and documents. Creating your online information service could be a lot easier than you might think. You may put a report or eBook into your terms. This is not plagiarism, but it is always finished. How long is it going to take? A day or two! A day or two!

Do so well... and you might have the best seller on your hands (and it is indeed a lovely thing!). In this post, I go over these freedoms.

c) Build Computer Products Again, and you need your computer to meet a need or promote or boost your future life. You will not have to write code, or you can pay to build it on your computer. I have a bunch of hard drive software programs that I have for free... why? But I am on the list of technology owners! Another way to market your software is to have a free version (to see how good it is free) with a paid version... works like a charm!

d) Ads Have you got a lot of traffic to your site? Sell ads like single ads, classified ads, etc. Right now, a prevalent advertisement medium.

When you write and publish eBooks, you can sell space for ads. Or, of course, you can advertise your product or service, or partner products... which makes sense to me — using Google AdSense or any other personalized ads provider. If you have a big popular website, you can receive a fair amount.

e) Open a Membership Page You're a niche expert. Will others want to know what you can share? If so, you could get your expertise paid monthly. Be mindful that you must keep the members paying on an ongoing basis month after month. You can also advise the members on other products or services and provide another revenue stream.

There are about as many ways to create passive digital revenue streams as your imagination can. Think outside.
Billions of dollars are invested every year online, set up your revenue streams, and get a slice of the pastry!

What Do You Need - Job or Passive Income?

JOB-What, the real people, do every day more than 80% PASSIVE INCOME-just for the dreamers, and it's wrong because the minority does it.

Work-Usually work for a company in a 3x4-meter cubicle, big enough to fit a desk and a chair. (except a managerial job where your own office is likely just as significant as your bedroom).

PASSIVE INCOME-Work wherever you want, be it at home, coffee shop, a house of friends, or even on the beach. JOB-Title speaks, when you work very hard, for several years, perhaps decades, you can appoint a sort of boss with a name and title sign sitting right in front of your desk for everyone to see. (sorry! -no managerial title means no office.) By the way, a management term typically has more responsibilities, more hours of work, and a salary increase.

PASSIVE INCOME–I'm sorry, you won't have a management name-who will handle you? As with house, name, and job, forget about it - you must stay in the comfort of your home with both the ocean on a sunshine bed or, worse case, your living room or workplace.

JOB-The paycheck rises each month, every 1 to 2 years, typically inflation-dependent. The rise is generally equivalent to or less than inflation when you work for a company that knows how to make a profit!!!

I almost forgot to mention that in times of economic recession such as the current, no annual income test increase usually occurs and even reduces often. You may lose your job in the worst case, but don't worry, there are always other jobs you can try to find.

PASSIVE INCOME-No assured monthly check, but you can play later if you work correctly now. Because you do for yourself and want this passive income by network marketing, internet marketing, or other strategies, the more time you use, the more money you have. An employer can't fire you the right thing because you're your boss. When things aren't working in a work area, have the correct thinking and persistence, you will still find something to do and set your goals for success.

JOB–In regular work, you can get a holiday leave from 25 to 35 working days per year covered either by your company or social insurance. What sounds okay? Sometimes you are forced to list the days you want to leave 2 or 3 months ahead because there are many employees and must plan a vacation schedule. If you can expect so much forward, but sometimes the unexpected happens, and your boss will probably decline any adjustments to your holiday schedule.

PASSIVE INCOME–Working for yourself and collecting your passive income ensures that you can take off on a day that you like or even the whole week off-who cares; your excess income helps pay the bills. You set your working schedule and your play schedule, and you have no supervisor who can refuse unpredictable applications.

JOB–Make sure that your alarm clock works so that you wake up ready for work the night, because if you don't know on time who's going to wait at the entrance-right, the boss!!! But, when it comes to finishing work when you stay for a couple of hours for nonpaid over time, I'm confident the boss doesn't care.

PASSIVE INCOME-No alarm clock, no awakening early in the morning even if you were late in the evening, but mostly no boss who has a "Killer Look." You will see that passive income stream if you realize that you are doing things properly–and you can give yourself the highest satisfaction and gratitude if you maintain your schedule and work hard following your strategy.

JOB–Work smarter and more challenging than anybody else, and you know what you're going to get–you thought it was a lot more work to do. Who cares, you'll see that you're the hard worker in the company (which sometimes isn't good because people are very jealous). However, the more difficult it gets, the more mistakes you make. Then guess who's going to "appreciate" all your mistakes–you know it, the boss!!!

PASSIVE INCOME-Work intelligently and more than any other person in your field, and your success is guaranteed. Sure on your trip, you will make mistakes, but for instance, you will have a team and a partner in the network companies that will direct you along the way (if you succeed, then they will grow too, so it is a win-win in the situation for all). On the other hand, errors will only motivate you to improve your job if you are your boss and the only person to blame, are you!!!

JOB–Work 40 hours a week for forty years, and you may get the golden look to show your grandkids how hard you worked in your life.

PASSIVE INCOME-Work for 40 hours a week, ten years, and allow you and your family to purchase as many watches and jewelry, and accessories as you like. The best part, though, is that you can travel with your grandchildren and friends because you share your money with them for your dream holidays and spend as much time and energy with them as you want.

JOB–Once you collect your paycheck, all the taxes will be deducted before you even see a cent-you see, not hard work. Hey, by the way, the employer will also contribute to your retirement, and nowadays, if you have about 65, almost 70, you will have a huge pension to do anything your heart wants (if it pumps). Nonetheless, there can be a downside to this. Often people work for 40 odd years and find there's no pension waiting for them, or financial experts have lost a good piece of it. But don't worry, you can always depend on kids or grandkids to support you.

Go INCOME PASSIVE-Tax? Okay, I suppose we all must pay somehow, but there are many legitimate ways to spend a lot lower than everybody thinks. The advantage of being an entrepreneur or a member of a network team is that you have other connections that have different contacts. All people are willing to show at the right affordable price how they have paid fewer taxes than usual and all legit!!! The best thing is that when you get old, you will not rely on your pension to pay your bills. Hold the profits in and with the relevant connections and innovative ideas that require a retirement.

JOB– Once you collect your paycheck, all the taxes will be deducted before you even see a cent-you see, not hard work. Hey, by the way, the employer will also contribute to your retirement, and nowadays, if you have about 65, almost 70, you will have a huge pension to do anything your heart wants (if it pumps). Nonetheless, there can be a downside to this. Often people work for 40 odd years and find there's no pension waiting for them, or financial experts have lost a good piece of it. But don't worry, you can always depend on kids or grandkids to support you.

Go INCOME PASSIVE-Tax? Okay, I suppose we all must pay somehow, but there are many legitimate ways to spend a lot lower than everybody thinks. The advantage of being an entrepreneur or a member of a network team is that you have other connections that have different contacts. All people are willing to show at the right affordable price how they have paid fewer taxes than usual and all legit!!! The best thing is that when you get old, you will not rely on your pension to pay your bills. Hold the profits in and with the relevant connections and innovative ideas that require a retirement.

What then, is a regular job like most people or passive income?

CHAPTER SIX

How Amazon FBA Helps Entrepreneurs

Amazon FBA is an ideal way of ensuring that you can sell and deliver your goods directly to customers to don't have to think about the shipping and handling process. It can also benefit businesses with enough storage space for their interests if they house the products on site. That said, Fulfillment By Amazon is the best part for every seller. Until you sign up, it is advised that you can control the process and the plan's scalability by deciding how your services meet your clients.

The number one component that you can consider when selling Fulfillment By Amazon is how your products reach customers at Amazon Prime. When using Amazon FBA, all the customers with an Amazon Prime account can choose two free delivery days. Along with Prime subscribers, Amazon regular customers will enjoy free delivery of $35.00 or more orders. One of FBA's main advantages is that the goods are advertised without shipping to Amazon Prime customers to increase sales.

What is Amazon FBA Core Seller?

The Amazon FBA Seller Central is a function of the Amazon website that you can use to monitor your items' warehousing, pricing of your products, and how your goods' selling features are displayed. Essentially, it is a whole website devoted to your services and how the public views them. You can search for your rights when added, check the other competing FBA sellers' prices, and see how you can proceed, such as delivering the products. Seller Central is essential for the sales process, as it gives the consumers the "first impression" when they discover your goods.

What is Amazon FBA Scalability?

The essential factor to consider when interacting with Amazon is the scalability of Amazon FBA. When your business grows, you want Amazon to expand with you to ensure that every order is carried out effectively. With the program's scalability, you can be confident that Amazon will support you through peak seasons and provide more resources if you sell more products. The options are endless, with the ability to pack and ship only one unit or thousands of companies.

The Amazon FBA Program

To begin, the Amazon FBA system stands for Amazon Completion. This is a service offered by Amazon that allows online and offline retailers to send their goods to Amazon. Amazon will deliver the items on your behalf to individual customers. If you don't visit regularly, you may not know how large the Amazon market is. They've come a long way from selling only books to selling almost anything now.

You can also sell products on Amazon and not use their FBA program so that you deliver your products, but the FBA system has many advantages, which frees up your time and provides a more streamlined business solution.

It is a product that other drop shippers have, but Amazon has its products in one of its centers. The company will deliver your goods on your behalf anytime and anywhere. You can further combine this program with your website and create an almost fully automated process to deliver Amazon and Amazon to its customers. The service cost is meager, and you only pay for your processing and delivery, and they do not charge a fee to use the platform at discount rates from Amazon.

So why should you consider using the platform of Amazon?

Here are some of the critical points in the FBA system:
-You can almost sell anything on Amazon or via your platform and pack it and send it.

-Automating your website with Amazon means you can run an autopilot company and take your time if you choose and still work for your company.

-Send the entire stock to Amazon, and all they'll do is to earn money.

Is now overstepping eBay for traffic on Alexa; they're a big eBay rival.

-Some eBay sellers use the Amazon FBA to deliver goods sold through eBay.

To learn how to start using this system and create online income streams. They give you all the necessary information about getting started. As I said before, you can sell practically anything. Amazon has eBay-like categories, for example, books that cover anything you can think of for home, garden, office, clothes, sports, etc.

Because of the FBA system and the considerable traffic created by Amazon, you can create an Amazon website, find items to sell, and run online with the resources they provide very quickly.

AMAZON PRODUCT LISTING DESCRIPTIONS

Amazon FBA has rapidly become a golden opportunity for various vendors and sells products on the Amazon website, both of whom have been in the early stages and willing to build an audience that desired what they were selling.

To do this correctly, you must precisely see what you are doing concerning the selling and displaying items.

Apart from beautiful images, the explanation is the crucial way people can understand what the product does, how it operates, and how it differs from other competing products.

This guide aims to highlight how you can handle the most convincing explanations of Amazon products...

The trick is straightforward, concise, and detailed if you want to create a useful collection.

The best usually have simple, high-definition photos paired with concise and informative newsletters (which concentrate on benefits) and a keyword-rich name.

The real murderer used the "print" in the catalog. The bullet points and the complete explanation allow you to explain the product's advantages while ensuring that the consumer is obligated to purchase your development as a fine line.

Because of the quality of this version, a variety of copywriting experts has paid for the provision of copywriting services "Amazon Product Listing." The idea is to help people make more money by writing a better version.

As mentioned above, the above structure defines quite a bit of whether Amazon approves an item.

What "triggers" consumers to trust the brand is the most important thing to do.

It's much better to deal with emotion than logic when selling products.

You can logically think that you can describe the item, and people will choose it, assess and purchase it based on its characteristics.

Emotionally, people select products they feel will bring their experience as close as possible to their aspirations.

For example, developing a convincing name (which lists the different characteristics of the product from how it can use it) and a summary explaining how the product will work into the consumer's life reflects much more than merely listing product features. Notice that most people purchase the drug for an additional reason... Highlighting how this underlying outcome can motivate them to make the difference between buying the item or not.

To an inevitable end, this illustrates how each element of the Description works: title The most important thing with the title of a product is that it is as descriptive as possible.

Clearly-there is no need for excessively detailed names for specific items (like books). Some classes, however, require the most concise signature possible.

Among 100's wash of similar products, customers need reliability, price, and confidence that the business behind the work will be legitimate. One of the best ways to do it is to have a definition, including the top some.

Pictures Images are required to identify things.
Clarity is* all*-don't think about backgrounds or anything-people would like to see the quality of the product and expect picture 4k+ to display it only shows what's needed-software products don't "need" a box but will contribute to its performance understanding—people need to see mainly screenshots to ensure the images reflect* exact*

Instead, there are sites like Fiverr that can also make a good shot.

The point is that while you have ~5 perfect images, this should be all right.

Features (bullet points) That's where things get high.

The functions (bullet points) are intended to describe the product specifications; now, they are mainly used to provide users with product information (copy).

Whatever you write there, there are several factors: wrap features within advantages-rather than saying "15 cm length," say "3 HANDY SIZES–5 cm, 10 cm & 15 cm." Include all five blocks, and it could be a temptation to use only 3–use all of these five and talk about the last one, with "CAPITALIZED," the buyers want to understand what the product is intended for. Amazon people buy things, don't know how the oven glove can make them look younger, etc.

As mentioned earlier, you must encourage customers to trust your business–and under your goods, build an effective system.

The way you do this is to make the most of the content available.

Definition Ultimately, the definition is most of the content below all "over fold" requirements.

The "definition" category may be several different items, depending on the type of product and whether you have a new brand or existing business.

It's best to look like an eBay product listing site-showing just what is for sale. A similar situation exists (you can use limited amounts of HTML in it) minus photos.

The most important thing is that you are not limited to bullet points only (as you are with the product features)-not only gives you a little more creative freedom. This means you must make sure you make the right choices...

Begin with the SINGLE reason why you would buy your product through rival-sales / advertising 101, but you can forget it so quickly.

As well as ratings, the way you show your item is essential.

Clarity is* all*-don't think about backgrounds or anything-people would like to see the quality of the product and expect picture 4k+ to display it only shows what's needed-software products don't "need" a box but will contribute to its performance understanding—

people need to see mainly screenshots to ensure the images reflect* exact*

Instead, there are sites like Fiverr that can also make a good shot.

The point is that while you have ~5 perfect images, this should be all right.

Features (bullet points) That's where things get high.

The functions (bullet points) are intended to describe the product specifications; now, they are mainly used to provide users with product information (copy).

Whatever you write there, there are several factors: wrap features within advantages-rather than saying "15 cm length," say "3 HANDY SIZES–5 cm, 10 cm & 15 cm." Include all five blocks, and it could be a temptation to use only 3–use all of these five and talk about the last one, with "CAPITALIZED," the buyers want to understand what the product is intended for. Amazon people buy things, don't know how the oven glove can make them look younger, etc.

As mentioned earlier, you must encourage customers to trust your business–and under your goods, build an effective system.

The way you do this is to make the most of the content available.

Definition Ultimately, the definition is most of the content below all "over fold" requirements.

The "definition" category may be several different items, depending on the type of product and whether you have a new brand or existing business.

It's best to look like an eBay product listing site-showing just what is for sale. A similar situation exists (you can use limited amounts of HTML in it) minus photos.

The most important thing is that you are not limited to bullet points only (as you are with the product features)-not only gives you a little more creative freedom. This means you must make sure you make the right choices...

Begin with the SINGLE reason why you would buy your product through rival-sales / advertising 101, but you can forget it so quickly.

As well as ratings, the way you show your item is essential.

Simple Start with Amazon FBA!

Amazon developed something called Amazon delivery, which operates much like eBay, but it is MUCH better.

eBay was the only place for some time to sell stuff online. eBay is good but requires a lot of effort from you: sourcing, listing, delivery, customer support, etc. If you plan to sell online, you can find Amazon's FBA fulfillment system. FBA means "Amazon's fulfillment," making it a fulfillment agency. A completing company offers processing and distribution services for the goods of its customers. FBA is different because Amazon is the marketplace for these products to sell the products actively. That makes FBA even more impressive because its goods also qualify for Amazon's delivery deals, including Free Super Saver Delivery and Amazon Prime.

It is essential to understand how FBA operates and how other organizations use FBA.

Buyers from Amazon use Prime to get free shipping. We spend much more on food, coffee, tea, socks, toilet paper, soap, detergent, and so on. They spend a lot more because they trust Amazon. This is great for buyers as it means you're going to make more and sell more.

Amazon is an internet business leader and has set high standards for its buyers, vendors, and owners. Customer service is essential to them, and they use Fulfillment from Amazon to do so. After the sale, you, as the product seller, no longer have to deal with customer service. You give more items to Amazon, and they take care of the rest.

This chapter will only cover your Amazon FBA account. We will submit your products more to Amazon, store and deliver your products to Amazon and handle your FBA stock in future articles.

1. Create an Amazon Account If you've never bought or sold an account on Amazon and do not have an account, go to Amazon's website and click on the Sales to Amazon link at the bottom of any page.

2. Call the Amazon customer service department to set up your FBA account once you have an Amazon purchase account. With a dedicated FBA representative on your account, you will be able to deal with all future problems. The rep will move through your first shipment.

So, if you get that far, the first due diligence is completed, and you have an FBA account.

Moneymaking in Amazon

Amazon has many products for buyers and sellers alike. But the best way to profit from an online retail platform is to be a customer and learn how to earn money from Amazon.

But what a website of your own? Then, you can begin your e-business with a 1-click order from Amazon.

It is as simple as uploading your goods and placing their cost and voila through Amazon's products advertisements, which expose your products to millions of online shoppers! Having it is for the world! This program requires a minimum of costs, allows you to traffic more on your site, and increases your chances of higher income by using more hits and clicks.

If your company is more service-oriented than your products, a website that offers a group of services marketed alongside your products also provides.

Another way to maximize money making in Amazon is through its service Fulfillment by Amazon (FBA). It allows you to stock your goods at Amazon's distribution centers, prepare and deliver them securely and directly, and offer quality customer service in your name.

No other website as a retailer can guarantee that your transactions are exact. Still, these services ensure that fraud can be identified and confirmed by Checkout by Amazon, Amazon Simple Pay, and Amazon Flexible Transactions and enable your customers to access the safest and most trustworthy online payment solution.

Amazon has plenty to give, whether you are an author or a member of the Amazon group of companies, CreateSpace, which offers a fast, simple, and cost-effective way to publish your content on the website and share it with potential customers on Amazon.com and other platforms.

As a programmer, the multitude of programs available on your websites, such as Advertising Web Services (API), Marketplace Web Services, Amazon website, Amazon Web Services, Completeness Web Services, Mechanical Turk, and Amazon Flexible Payments will improve your productivity.

All these affiliate programs make your e-commerce more up-to-date and customer-friendly by making it possible for developers to create new and innovative ways of handling business by clicking on a button. They contain all the resources you need to update your page to make payment more comfortable and accessible.

There are several ways to make money from Amazon's online retail platform and items that emerging entrepreneurs and old school business people may do to look for a new way to move their companies. All it takes is a couple of minutes.

CHAPTER SEVEN

What does drop shipping mean?

It's a way of selling items to your customers without keeping your stock. You just let the supplier know when an order has been placed, and they will ship to the customer directly.

It can be very efficient and easy to do. That's the way many eBay Power Sellers work. However, it can be challenging to find the right suppliers, so most people use a wholesale drop shipping directory to find quality and reliable suppliers.

To create passive income streams on the internet, most individuals use drop shipping. You've probably heard of people living from eBay making their full-time living. Perhaps, many people are checking out local garage sales, picking up some things, and selling them online. But most people who make big money don't see the goods they're making. They don't even pay in advance for them.

Dropshipping is becoming an effortless way for people to benefit from home without any cash start-up in their spare time.

The definition is easy to grasp, but when you need to find a supplier, the hard part comes. This move is crucial and will decide how much money you're making. You need to find a supplier that sells your product at a price you can make a profit. It may seem like an impossible task if you don't know where to look.

Do what most people do-look for distributors in drop ship and retail directories if you want to save yourself time and headache. Such lists compile suppliers in one location, actual and sometimes pre-screened (depending on the list), so users can easily browse through to find those that meet their needs.

You will be able to compare rates with your membership, read reviews, and see other people's experiences to ensure the supplier is legit. Online scams have caught a lot of people. Don't let that happen to you.

Additionally, many of these databases come with teaching materials and private forums, so you know you're not going to be alone if you ever need help or have any questions.

How to Start Dropshipping Successfully

Over the past few decades, the entire spectrum of doing business has experienced a lot of transition. Dropship services are one of the latest online business ideas. This online business requires a process in which producers or distributors supply the products directly to the dropship business customers without buying or storing them in advance. The best part of the deal is that no hard work, such as inventing, designing, purchasing, and producing the product, checking the demand, presenting the effect on the internet, making the website appealing, or selling the product, has to be done by the business owner or reseller.

The business owner of drop-ship services has to list the products on eBay and get orders for the products using the specifications and graphics of their own or the distributor firm. The reseller provides information on the names and addresses of the customers and other specifics of the order when the orders are issued so that the manufacturer can deliver the goods to the customer. The client also receives the fee.

The market of dropship service may yield rich returns for the small businessman. Still, the most significant drop shipping guide is that it is necessary to take care of the company and customers and ensure that any purchaser's concerns about poor product performance or delays between receiving payments and delivering goods are promptly tendentious. It is vital to choose a reliable supplier to answer how to dropship and begin a dropshipping company. False selection can result in disastrous results. Before starting this type of business, follow the following steps.

1) Choose Recommended Suppliers: The first step to begin the business of drop-ship services should select suppliers very carefully—select other people's suggested suppliers. Lists of drop shipping companies can be downloaded free or charged on Internet directory pages. Most have accurate information, while unscrupulous vendors may operate others, so avoid such specific recommendations.

2) Check the contact information: once a choice has been made based on credible advice and ensuring that the supplier provides the range of products that the client wants to work with, check the supplier's contact details. Relevant contact information such as telephone number, email address, and mailing address should be available on the supplier's website. Remove any company that has inaccurate or no contact information at all. Make sure the phone is answered and see how long it takes the manufacturer to respond to emails, which may be useful later if you have a reason to contact them with a question.

3) Check the supplier's terms and conditions: because there may be conflicts with the supplier regarding faulty products or non-delivered goods, the supplier's terms and conditions should be appropriately specified and understood by the reseller. Realize that the company's obligations are different from the distributor's duties towards the reseller.

4) Unreasonable subscription charges: the dropship services company as a reseller must pay reseller registration fees and, in some cases, continuing subscription fees for the right of access to the supplier's catalog. Access is usually allowed before registration for a limited time. Test to see if it pays recurring subscription fees before registering with any supplier. We should carefully check fine printing for any clauses between the lines.

5) Beware of intermediaries Disguised as suppliers: check that the prospective supplier has enough inventory of the goods and that they are not intermediaries posing as suppliers. Such intermediaries place orders with the actual supplier, and there may be extended delays when they obtain warrants from the reseller. Such delays can result in losses to the consumer and subsequent failure to the reseller due to the fee's repayment.

6) Payment methods: find out how the manufacturer wants payments to be collected as the most convenient method would be the same as the customer's payment method. This will save money and costs. It is also best to avoid paying for Telegraph Transfer or Wire Transfer because if there is no consumer service, the risk is higher.

7) Look out for companies selling fake goods: avoid such sites offering branded goods such as designer clothing or electrical goods at incredibly low prices when selecting a manufacturer. These low-priced, so-called designer products are likely to be counterfeit unless the manufacturer is renowned and trustworthy. The goods are purchased from a close-out, or if the goods are refurbished or returns from Grade A. If the dealer sells fake products, **may charge** him with selling counterfeit goods.

8) Search for Online Reviews: after a few suppliers have been shortlisted, it would be useful to check for reviews and suggestions from other dropship resellers on the Internet forums. Although it may be hard to find any good comments as resellers do not want others to know about their lucrative origin, bad reviews will certainly help make the right decision.

9) Search for artists and artisans: a unique way to do drop-ship services business is to team up with artists and artisans for their creative goods. Generally, these creative people lack knowledge of advertising. Visits to local trade fairs will offer unlimited opportunities to buy unique original products at incredibly low prices compared to eBay prices. Such products do not need to be purchased by the drop ship company, but an agreement could be made to work on commission. We will probably be happy when a sale is made to the dropship business buyer to take his fee and deliver the goods.

Understanding Basic Affiliate Marketing

Understanding Affiliate Marketing Affiliate Marketing is an online term used to describe internet business promotion by distributing affiliate programs and marketing these goods on websites and dates to the mid-1990s. The distributor compensates the affiliate (also known as the publisher) for an acceptable percentage of profit based on the amount of trade their w.

Some businesses like Clickbank, Paydotcom, and Shareasale have typically set percentage rates for partners that can be as high as 75 percent for items. Many find ads based on commissions to be a form of revenue sharing or another term commonly used.

Associated it.in the early days of "affiliate marketing" as another network marketing or multi-level marketing (MLM) structure, and as a result of this misconception, allotment of online businesses decided to use the term "performance marketing" to avoid any relationship with affiliate marketing. This also created a big problem for affiliates in the past, as many online users were inclined to frown on anything.

The Benefits of Affiliate Marketing For some time now, the revenue sharing model has been around, allocating more than online business and the internet. But the concept of affiliate marketing brought it to new levels and became an essential form of advertising and activity for all e-commerce forms. Internet marketers find affiliate advertising particularly attractive because it poses little or no threat to both the retailer and the' affiliate.' This is how it all works. The affiliate can earn money if the companion takes to the merchant's website, either through online links on the affiliate's website or via email, forums, RSS feeds, and many other online communications.

Accounts canceled if you create what is considered to be an IP address.

What are the distinctive types of affiliate marketing? May an affiliate receive commissions online in a few different ways? First, you need to determine which of these is correct for you and then enter the affiliate partner program to make any fee through any referrals from your website to the retailer. Here are four approaches used online today, however. You need to read the terms and conditions of each affiliate program you wish to join.

Pay Per Click Advertising is essentially a tactic that affiliates use when content is advertised on their affiliate page and is then charged when a customer clicks on that website ads, whether it is a text connection or photo link.

Emailing your subscription lists with your affiliate reference embedded "Spam Is Not Tolerated" guarantees that you review the affiliate program's TOS before doing so.

CPA Affiliate Marketing is portrayed and promoted through this marketing form when one website visitor interacts with a specific website, whether it is a free newsletter or subscription.

Shareasale, Paydotcom, and Clickbank are all affiliate marketing networks with thousands of products and services to choose from and are free to join. Several systems also make it possible to set up multi-tier or what is called a periodic payment system.

Ideally, this book has helped you better understand affiliate marketing, and we would like to wish you well in all your online businesses.

Affiliate Marketing VS Product Creation

Once entering the online marketing world, most people face a significant obstacle: should I become an affiliate marketer, or should I build and sell my product?

Before I start, let me define the two business models quickly to clear how money is generated with each one.

- **Affiliate Marketing:** You can earn income in this business model by referring consumers to another person's product or service. So you'll permanently sign up as an associate with the vendor and get paid a fee for every sale you make.
- **Product Creation:** This business plan is quite self-explanatory; you will create a product and sell it on the market for 100% of the profits. We will presume in this instance that your service is some knowledge item.

Many marketers will say that affiliate advertising is the best way to start making money online. Just because you can choose a vendor whose brand you want to endorse, sign up as an affiliate, start sending traffic to the sales page of your companion, and BOOM! You're gaining capital. It sounds simple. You don't have to deal with creating a product, setting up websites, dealing with customers, etc. At the same time, some marketers say it's easier and more profitable to make your product and allow you to have more control over your company.

It all depends on your strengths and weaknesses and what you want your company to achieve.

Let me get some of everyone's pros and cons to put things in perspective so you can get a better idea of where you want to get going.

Here are some of the affiliate marketing pros:

- Most affiliate vendors/networks are free and readily available. Most of the time, you're going to answer a couple of basic questions, set up a username and password, and get instant access to the affiliate member area within minutes.

- Products for advertising are given. When you set up your profile in the affiliate member region, you'll have full access to all the marketing materials you need to get started, including banners, pre-written emails, etc. You will also obtain a special affiliate connection in the member's area that will bring your prospects to a full sales site that has already been developed for you. All you need to concentrate on is getting visitors to your affiliate page with these products.

- You already have all the websites made for you. You don't have to deal with the distractions that may come with setting up a website as an affiliate. The vendor has done this for you, and your purchases and fees will be tracked through this page and charged into your account as long as you use your affiliate card.

- You don't have to deal with clients. We all know how hard it can be to deal with customers, but you don't have to think about this topic as an affiliate. When you make an affiliate purchase, all you need to think about is cash your check and passing the customer on to the seller.

As you will see, it certainly has its advantages as an affiliate marketer. Joining a vendor/network is quick and easy. All marketing materials and sales pages are given, and you don't have to deal with clients. You can concentrate your time on traffic generation, sales, and cashing checks!

Now let's look at some of the affiliate marketing drawbacks and how you can solve them.

- The match. While I could claim affiliate marketing as the easiest way to make money online, I can strongly argue that it is the most difficult because of the competition. You must deal with hundreds of thousands of affiliate marketers to make a sale. At the same time, most seasoned marketers believe that most new affiliate marketers don't know what they're doing because getting into it is such an accessible business.

Educating yourself is one of the easiest ways to overcome this challenge. Always be a step ahead of the contest by learning what the top affiliates are doing to give them the edge they need to sell.

- Use margins. You are paying a profit to refer a buyer to a seller as opposed to you being the maker of the service and receiving 100% of the revenue, as I described before with affiliate marketing. So you can leave a lot of money on the table by endorsing the brand of someone else instead of your own. This challenge is not really in your control when it comes to advertising partners, but the best thing you can do is promote a product with a higher payout of 60-80% compared to 25-50%. This way, with fewer sales, you can make more money.
- You are building a business for someone else. Not only do you produce sales and profits for the supplier as an associate, but you also help them develop their company rather than your own. When

you make a deal, and a fee is paid, the customer is now in the vendor's hands that can continue to sell more products and services to that customer for their relationship's lifetime.

The best way to build your own company through affiliate marketing while also sending customers to the retailer is to set up your landing page, which involves the prospect of entering your name and email before accessing the sales site. As a result, the opportunity is also on your customer list, and you can now email them directly to future offers and affiliate products. Now, of course, you'll need to allow them to enter their address, such as giving away a free document, video training, audio file, etc. In a future record, we will discuss this.

• Missing command. You don't have much power over anything but producing revenue through affiliate marketing. If the network/vendor wants to shut down or sell the product you are selling, square one is left behind. You have a lot more control over the business when it comes to brand development and can make profits, but we're going to be touching on that in a moment.

This is a significant downside to affiliate marketing, sadly, and something you can't plan for. As described above, creating your email list is the best way to guarantee that you can still generate business with your existing customer list when setting up a new campaign with a new product.

There are just as many negatives to affiliate marketing as benefits, but none of these factors will keep you from starting if it is a company you want to pursue. One important thing you want to keep in mind is to take time to put yourself ahead of the curve in your education and skillsets. By doing this, you are separating yourself from the competition and making the selling a leap forward.

Visit my author's toolbox if you are keen to learn more about affiliate marketing and jumping from your way to success.

Now, just for a second picture, you are the product creator, and you have an army of affiliates that promote your products as we move into the pros and cons of creating and selling your product.

Product creation Product development can be a frightening topic for many because, as a newbie, you are most likely uncertain about how an online business operates, let alone designing a product from scratch, and totally in the dark. Yet it can be one of the simplest ways to make money online to your delight.

Let's get into some of the pros of creating and selling your product and see why you feel it can be an avenue:

- Power. You are in complete control of just about everything when it comes to brand development. You oversee how you sell your service, the cost, its distribution, and you are in complete control of every customer you bring into your company and any potential transactions that you make.

- Profits. This is, of course, a significant reason why many people are creating and selling their products. You will retain 100 percent of the profits from every sale you make as a brand maker. Now, when it comes to setting up your affiliate program and making other affiliates market your goods, there is an exception to that, but we will focus on the impact of this next one.

- Leaders. You may choose to influence others to help build your business once you produce your unique product. Establishing an affiliate program can be a powerful way to explode your autopilot business. You can offer a commission of 30-50 percent to your affiliates and have them sell off their asses for you, especially if your product brings high value to the marketplace. You can also make money while you're sleeping while your partners work hard to make you sell.

- Design of a product. Being the product maker allows you to create your brand on your chosen topic's marketplace. You can call the product whatever you like and build a brand around that theme because your work is different. If you want to develop your company with word-of-mouth marketing that we all know is the best advertising form, this is very high.

As you can see, making and selling your service also has some significant advantages. You're in full control of everything, earning more money, building an army of partners, and building a brand for yourself and your company. But as there's a downside in everything, so let's get into the next one.

Here are some of the drawbacks of brand development and how to solve them: • Time. When it comes to your money, it will take more of your time to create your service and then sign up as an affiliate. It will not only take time to complete your product, but you must also create a website from which to sell your product. And that can be his headache that we're going to talk about next.

The great thing about creating a product is that you can outsource just about any process that starts your business. To write the data service for you, you can pay a professional writer and take the credit for it. You always want to read it and change it a little to suit your personality and style, of course.

Web pages. Once you've finished your work, you won't be able to make any profit unless you can get it published online. This may be the worst fear for some. This can cause you a lot of headaches, particularly if you're not knowledgeable about tech. This can easily cause you to leave or never continue trying to make money online, or it can cause you to have to hire a web designer to create a website that can cost you a few hundred to a few thousand dollars. This takes me to my next subject.

Can conveniently outsource the construction of a web site to a web designer who can typically build a clean, professional website within 48-72 hours.

- Price. Can safely say that when it comes to creating a company, you will have more start-up costs than an associate. Don't worry about taking a deep breath. Many of the things you're going to pay for are cheap. For about $10, you can buy a domain, and it's about $5 a month to host. Now I want to bring you to a platform that is called Fiverr that will radically change the way you do business. This is a people's community willing to do just about anything for $5. Go ahead and see for yourself on the web.

You can create an information item on a subject of your choosing, design the graphics and ebook cover, and develop a website for $25-$30.

- Help for customers. You will be responsible for your customer service and support as the brand owner, and this alone will drive you crazy and waste a great deal of your time and energy. You'll have your happy customers and your not-so-happy customers as in any company on or off-line. Your consumers will have queries, suggestions, complaints, etc. It is your responsibility to ensure that they receive the support they deserve.

It can also outsource customer support, but sadly, this has to do with any company area and something you'll contend with. Yes, you can get someone to take care of your customer service, but you certainly need to be as proactive as possible to make sure they get the best possible help.

As you can see as a company holder, yes, you're going to be in charge, yes, you're going to make more money, and yes, you're going to be able to build a brand, but with all that comes a lot more responsibility than a marketer.

Until wrapping up stuff, let's focus on some issues we can all agree on in affiliate marketing and brand development.

- Homework. Whether you're an affiliate marketer or you're selling your goods, you can both monitor your time and work from home. This is a highly sought-after privilege for many to spend more time with relatives, friends, spouses, etc. Unless you're a professional marketer, and you've been born with excellent online business skills, most of you will still be focusing on your day job while developing your business online. That said, you can build your online business on a part-time or full-time basis around your current schedule of work, whether it's an hour a day or ten hours a day, whatever works for you to make sure you keep it consistent. Make sure you arrange your business online like you prepare any other event and make it non-negotiable.

- You're the boss. You are your boss in both cases, regardless of whether you are selling as an agent or your service, and your efforts directly influence your revenue. This also makes it possible for you to make money on demand. You can hop on your computer and set up a new marketing campaign if you're looking to take a trip or buy a new car and you need a few thousand dollars.

CONCLUSION

If you are more inclined to make your items, please visit my toolbox for the author.

To conclude, there is no right or wrong, better or worse; that was not this chapter's point. This report aimed to shed some light on both business models so you could be more aware of what you can expect in your online business going forward. I don't think there should be a choice between advertising partners and making your brand. You should both build into your business plan and train yourself in both arenas. By doing so, you can soon see that many top affiliate marketers are making a killing selling their goods, and many people selling their products are making a killing as affiliate marketers.

No matter what you do, I want to emphasize that it will take time, commitment, and hard work. Do not fall into the trap of many newbies doing that is continually searching for the next plug and play the system to make you the next millionaire overnight. And there's plenty of "Guru's" out there who are preying on the newbie crowd and throwing out fake items with pretty marketing pages that promise millions overnight, and you're still falling for them. STOP!! Map a business plan, determine what you want to do, find a reputable mentor, and get to work! Keep on following the mentor chosen to your first dollar online. Finally, give yourself a promise you won't quit until you start the journey!

CPSIA information can be obtained
at www.ICGtesting.com
Printed in the USA
LVHW050121120121
676232LV00030B/931